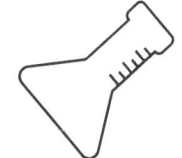

$A = b$

THE ULTIMATE ACTIVITY BOOK FOR
AWESOME TEACHERS

Sam Harris

ISBN: 978-1-64845-108-9

Copyright @ 2023 by LAK Publishing

All rights reserved. No part of this book may be reproduced, scanned, or distributed in any printed or electronic form without permission. Please do not participate in or encourage piracy of copyrighted materials in violation of the author's rights. Purchase only authorized editions.

CONTENTS

INTRODUCTION 5

ACTIVITIES 6

CONCLUSION 119

SOLUTIONS 120

INTRODUCTION

There's a wise old saying—claimed by some people to be the words of Benjamin Franklin, no less—that says that teaching is the only profession that actively creates all other professions.

It's a clever aphorism, certainly, but it's also completely true. Teachers are in an extraordinary situation, after all. Through their work, they have the opportunity to instil a love and enthusiasm for almost any subject in each of their students. And if that student so wishes, it could be that subject that then sets them on their path in life, and helps them to establish their place in the world.

Put like that, teaching seems a truly extraordinary job. But all that life-shaping and enthusiasm-instilling is not exactly easy, and as you will no doubt know, teaching comes with its fair share of responsibilities—as well as long days, and extra hours outside of the classroom marking, prepping, and researching at home.

But that is where this book comes in.

This is **The Ultimate Teacher Activity Book**. Inside here are more than 100 pages of puzzles, games, and trivia quizzes, all specially compiled to give you a much-needed break from your day-to-day work shaping the generations to come. Scattered throughout the book along the way are dozens of cartoons, jokes, wise words, and some tantalizing did-you-knows, all intended to provide some food for thought too.

So what are you waiting for? Get yourself a pen and a cup coffee (or something stronger, if you wish), put your feet up, and take your mind off it all with our very first game…

Some teachers are jacks and jills of all trades, while others are specialists in only one or two subjects. Which of these high school topics best suits you—and how many of them can you find in the wordsearch below?

- ART
- BIOLOGY
- CHEMISTRY
- COMPUTER SCIENCE
- DRAMA
- ECONOMICS
- ENGLISH
- FRENCH
- GEORGRAPHY
- HISTORY
- MATH
- MUSIC
- PHYSICS
- SOCIAL STUDIES
- SPANISH

```
C H F H V G Y Q E A H R L I T
K G H A C G E C O R E G C F K
A Y Q T O N O O K T J Z O P H
Q M S L A N E S R A B X I L S
R H O Q O M X R C G A J L L I
P I K M O N V C F K R Y E J L
B R I H S I N A P S R A N B G
V C O A M A R D X D M C P U N
S Z N U A O Y V P N G X L H E
H I S T O R Y W C H P D K F Y
O I E F N D I Q K T Y F U D R
C H I S Q M C H E M I S T R Y
P O Q A F U S G P T Q H I A D
C O M P U T E R S C I E N C E
S O C I A L S T U D I E S Z S
```

In this acrostic puzzle, place the answers to the trivia questions into the corresponding rows in the grid below, and the name of something from a high school English lesson will be spelled out down the shaded column.

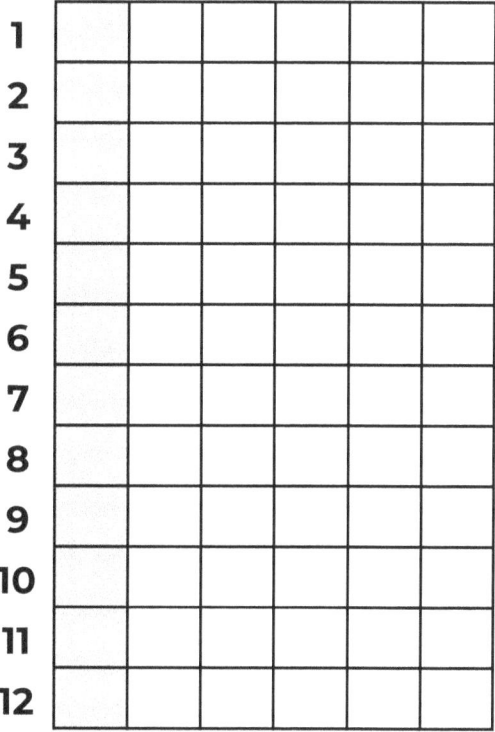

1. In the Bible, which prophet anointed Saul as king?

2. Which Russian psychologist is known for his work on the conditioned response?

3. Who invented the kinetoscope?

4. What measurement is equal to around 3 statute miles?

5. Which member of the Beatles (surname only) had the middle name Winston?

6. Who was the son of Daedalus in Greek mythology?

7. In what US state is Carson City?

8. What was the name of Queen Elizabeth II's father?

9. What river flows through London?

10. What is the Spanish name for Spain?

11. What is the sixth planet from the Sun?

12. What South Seas island in Polynesia is associated with the artist Paul Gauguin?

Complete this classic sudoku grid by filling in the numbers 1–9 so that each row, each column, and each smaller set of 3 x 3 squares contain each number just once and once only.

2			7			8	6	
8	6		2	4			3	5
1		4		3				2
	7	6	4	9				
					6		5	9
3		1						6
7					4		9	1
6				2			8	
9		8			7			3

DID YOU KNOW

May 7 is national Teacher Appreciation Day!

Five students—Aaron, Bryan, Charlie, Darren, and Eddie—are all late handing in their homework. Each student has a different excuse: one of them left it on the school bus; another left it at their grandmother's house; another says he had a stomachache last night; another thought it was for tomorrow; and another had his homework eaten by the dog (supposedly…!)

Based on the clues below, can you figure out which boy has which excuse?

1. The student who left his homework on the bus has a double letter in his name—as does the student with the stomachache, and the student who left his work at his grandmother's house!

2. The student with the longest name did not leave his work anywhere.

3. The student with the stomachache has a name ending in E.

4. The name of the student whose dog ate his homework is listed alphabetically immediately after the student who left his homework at his grandmother's house.

STUDENT	EXCUSE
Aaron	
Bryan	
Charlie	
Darren	
Eddie	

Can you find your way through this maze from one side to the other?

In this mini crossword, the answers are all anagrams of the clue words. Watch out, though—if there is more than one possible answer, you'll have to make sure you put the right one in the grid!

Across
1. REMIT → **TIMER**
6. QUALE → **EQUAL**
7. HEARS → **SHARE**
8. GLARE → **LARGE**
9. SPARK → **PARKS**
12. TRAIL → **TRIAL**
13. GREEN → **GENRE**
14. MOPES → **POEMS**

Down
1. SETT → **TEST**
2. GERANIUMS → **MEASURING**
3. LEER → **REEL**
4. VICTUALER → **LUCRATIVE**
5. EELS → **ELSE**
9. GAPE → **PAGE**
10. PETS → **STEP**
11. SILL → **ILLS**

T	I	M	E	R	■	L	■	E
E	■	E	■	E	Q	U	A	L
S	H	A	R	E	■	C	■	S
T	■	S	■	L	A	R	G	E
■	■	U	■	■	■	A	■	■
P	A	R	K	S	■	T	■	I
A	■	I	■	T	R	I	A	L
G	E	N	R	E	■	V	■	L
E	■	G	■	P	O	E	M	S

How many triangles are there in total in this shape?

How's your history knowledge? Listed on the left here are the names of eight famous historical figures. On the right, are years in which they died. Can you correctly match all eight pairs together? The first has been filled in to make a start...

ELIZABETH I ☐		☐ 1216
MARCO POLO ☐		☐ 1324
KING JOHN ☐		☐ 1431
CHARLES DICKENS ☐		☐ 1506
QUEEN VICTORIA ☐		☐ 1603
JOAN OF ARC ☐		☐ 1799
GEORGE WASHINGTON ☐		☐ 1870
CHRISTOPHER COLUMBUS ☐		☐ 1901

How about a classic quick crossword to keep you busy?

Across

1. Secrecy (7)
5. Pointed (5)
8. Oriental (7)
9. Separately (5)
10. Piquancy (5)
11. Ever-living (7)
12. Produce (6)
14. Repeated phrase (6)
17. Let go of (7)
19. Washed out, pallid (5)
22. See eye to eye (5)
23. First letter (7)
24. Requires (5)
25. Outcomes (7)

Down

1. Encounters (5)
2. Japanese dish (5)
3. Aspect of (7)
4. Over there (6)
5. Left over, unused (5)
6. Versus (7)
7. Kneecap (7)
12. Sure (7)
13. Make bigger (7)
15. Puts to use (7)
16. Older, elder (6)
18. Aids in a crime (5)
20. Unmoving (5)
21. Shouts (5)

Results day already! Can you fit these 15 test outcomes and schoolwork comments into the correct spaces in the grid below?

- A PLUS
- BETTER
- D MINUS
- DIPLOMA
- DISTINCTION
- FAIL
- HONOR ROLL
- MERIT
- MUCH IMPROVED
- MUST TRY HARDER
- OUTSTANDING
- PASS
- PERCENTILE
- TOP OF THE CLASS

Here's a quick test from US citizenship class. Ten of the answers in the grid below were members of the original 13 United States. The other five were not. Can you cross out the wrong answers, leaving only the ten correct founding states intact?

DELAWARE	NORTH DAKOTA	IDAHO
NEW YORK	NEW HAMPSHIRE	RHODE ISLAND
OHIO	SOUTH CAROLINA	GEORGIA
PENNSYLVANIA	MARYLAND	VIRGINIA
WASHINGTON	NORTH CAROLINA	VERMONT

Here's a tricky picture puzzle to get your brain around... Are there more music lessons, geography lessons, or drama lessons in the grid below?

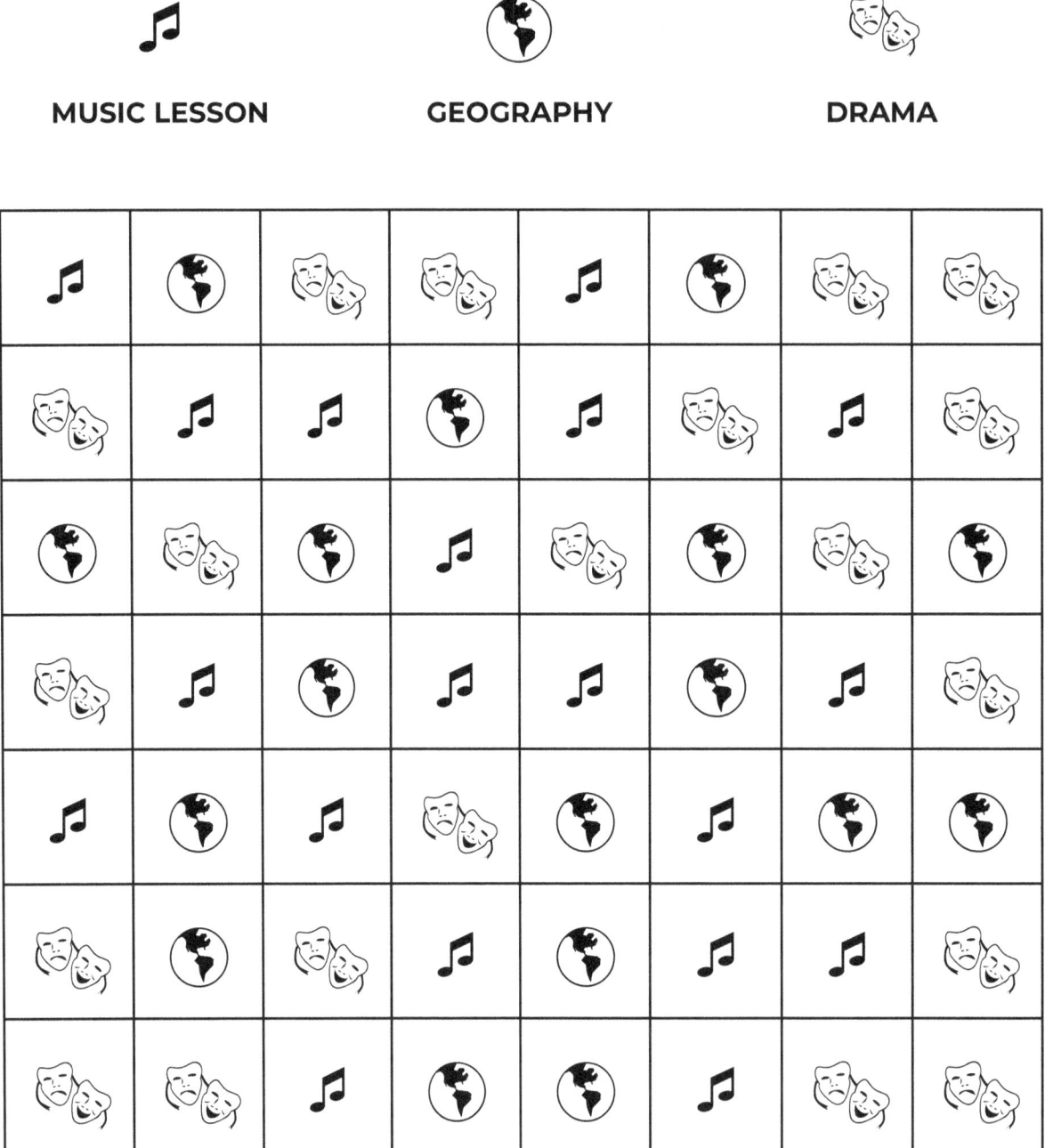

We're off to the drama department! The names of eleven parts of a stage and theatre are hidden in the grid below. Unlike an ordinary word search though, they're not in straight lines! Can you find all the answers, so that no letter is left over, and no letter is used more than once? The first has been filled in for you to make a start.

C	U	R	A	U	D	I	T	S	S
R	O	T	S	T	A	L	O	E	I
C	I	A	T	C	O	L	R	R	N
H	N	P	I	T	S	S	I	D	G
E	R	A	M	U	N	E	U	M	R
S	T	D	E	O	R	R	W	I	O
A	P	E	T	C	E	S	E	N	O
R	P	M	P	H	O	U	G	G	M
T	R	O	B	A	S	T	A	S	A
M	E	N	T	C	K	N	O	R	P

How many of these classic American novelists can you find in the grid below?

- ASIMOV
- BELLOW
- CHANDLER
- FAULKNER
- FITZGERALD
- HAWTHORNE
- HELLER
- KEROUAC
- MELVILLE
- MORRISON
- PLATH
- SALINGER
- STEINBECK
- UPDIKE
- WHITMAN

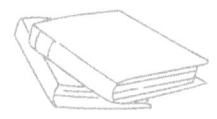

```
W D F A S O Y I S C M R X H E
R B L L S U U T G A O E Y A M
H E Y A P I E V N U R L G W Y
U K N D R I M A R O R D Z T O
E N I K N E M O Y R I N O H F
A K Y B L T G T V E S A B O R
E D E O I U L Z O K O H T R D
G C K H P L A K T L N C K N Q
K W W C A Y Z F R I W K I E I
M E L V I L L E Y K F N Q B U
H H P X L Q L H T A L P Y R Y
D J D B H L B R E G N I L A S
S X H R E Z E C M P K L E Q H
J W X H B E L L O W V Y Y W I
C D A L J J Q Z M U W E L Z L
```

It's parents' evening, and the parents of five students—Annie, Ben, Charles, Diedre, and Evie—have turned up to speak to the teachers of five different subjects: History, Art, Geography, Music, and Math.

Based on the clues below, can you figure out which student's parent is here to speak to which subject's teacher?

1. Neither of the two boys' parents are here to see the math tutor.

2. The student whose parents are here to speak to the head of geography has a name one letter longer than that of the student whose parents are here to speak to the math teacher.

3. Diedre's parents are here to see her music teacher...

4. ...but Charles' parents are not here to see the art teacher.

STUDENT	SUBJECT
Annie	
Ben	
Charles	
Diedre	
Evie	

Complete this classic sudoku grid by filling in the numbers 1–9 so that each row, each column, and each smaller set of 3 x 3 squares contain each number just once and once only.

4		6	9	5			8	3
				8	2		4	5	
			4	3			1	6
5	3	4		8			6	
		7	3					5
	2				5	1	3	
	1						7	8
	4	3					9	
6	8			9	3			1

> **DID YOU KNOW**
>
> The country with the highest number of primary teachers is China—with more than 6.6 million!

Starting at the 8 in the top left corner here, complete all the squares in the grid below using each of the calculations between them to fill in the gaps.

8	x2		+5		÷7	

x3 −25% +3 x10

| | ÷2 | | x2 | | +6 | |

x2 x5 +25% ÷2

| | +25% | 60 | ÷2 | | x0.5 | |

−8 −12 x2, +4 −7

| | +20% | | +16 | | √ = | |

23

Can you find your way through this maze from one side to the other?

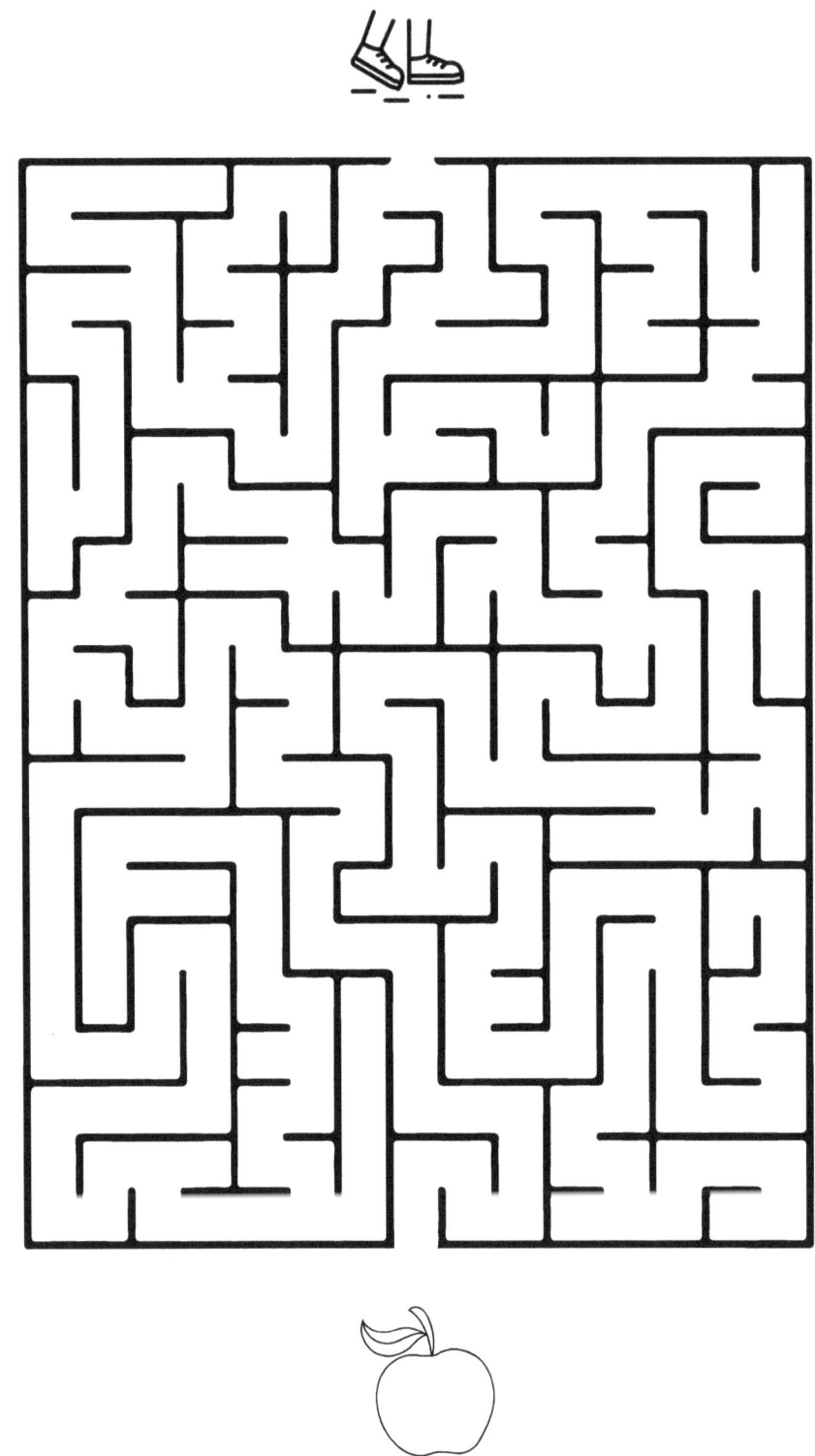

Two things you might find in a geography classroom—both of which have five letters in their name—have been jumbled together here. What are they?

Each of the 6-letter words below is missing a litter, which fits in the gap. Once all the words have been filled in, a two-word schoolyard phrase will read down the in central column. Watch out—there might be multiple possible answers to the missing letters, but only one correct solution overall!

E	A	**S**	T	E	R			
		C	O	O	L	E	R	
I	N	C	**H**	E	S			
T	O	R	P	**O**	R			
		M	**O**	V	I	N	G	
C	O	L	**L**	A	R			
			B	L	E	A	C	H
		R	**E**	S	I	G	N	
I	N	S	T	I	**L**			
			P	**L**	A	Y	E	R

26

Off to gym class! Listed on the left here are the names of eight items of sporting equipment. On the right, are sports in which they might be used. Can you correctly match all eight pairs together? The first has been filled in for you to make a start.

SHUTTLECOCK ☐	———	☐ Badminton
POMMEL HORSE ☐		☐ Cricket
MITT ☐		☐ Golf
CARABINER ☐		☐ Soccer
RACKET ☐		☐ Baseball
SHIN GUARD ☐		☐ Gymnastics
TEE ☐		☐ Climbing
BAILS ☐		☐ Tennis

Time to put your feet up for a few minutes in the staff room! Fit the 15 staff room items listed here into the grid below.

- ARMCHAIR
- BELL
- BOOKCASE
- CLOCK
- COFFEE MACHINE
- CUPBOARD
- FILE CABINET
- FIRST AID
- FRIDGE
- PHOTOCOPIER
- PLANTS
- WINDOW

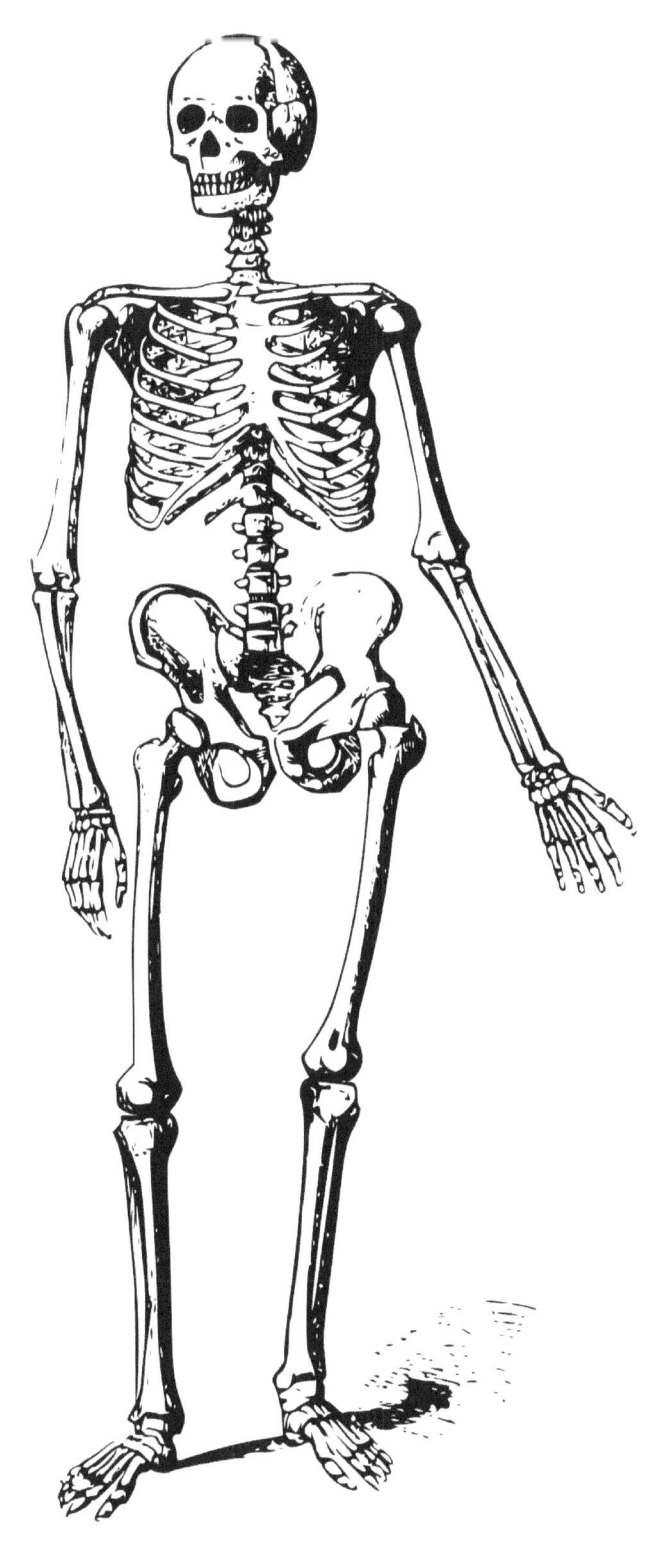

"I'M JUST GOING TO WAIT FOR YOU ALL TO BE QUIET."

Complete this classic sudoku grid by filling in the numbers 1–9 so that each row, each column, and each smaller set of 3 x 3 squares contain each number just once and once only.

		2	3				8	
4		1			6	7	2	
	5	8	2				1	
2	8					3	5	
	6			5	8	9		
	4			3	2		6	
	2		6		3			4
9	1			7		2		6
5	3					8	7	

> ☼ **DID YOU KNOW** ☼
>
> **The average age for a retiring teacher is 59—but that number is increasing!**

Place the answers to these trivia questions into the corresponding rows in the grid below, and the name of a piece of equipment from shop class will be spelled out down the shaded column.

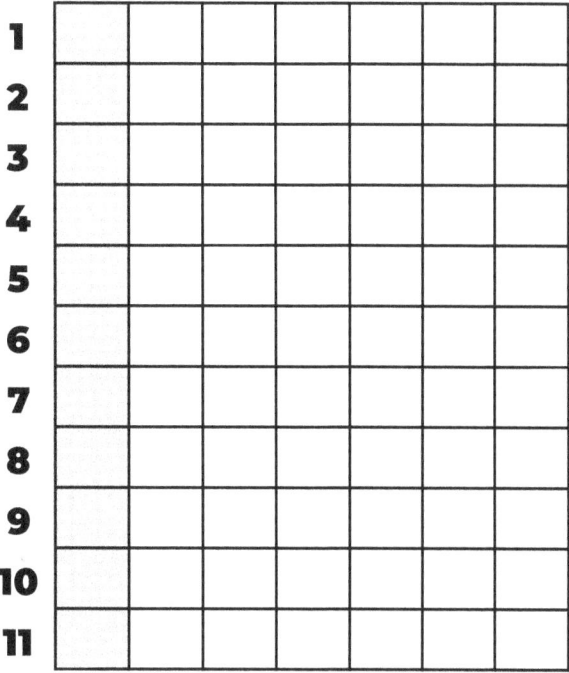

1. What is each of the numbered sections into which the books of the Bible are divided known as?

2. Piedmontese and Venetian are regional varieties of what European language?

3. What nationality was the author Boris Pasternak?

4. What is the largest city in Alberta?

5. Real-life descriptions of the rhinoceros are believed to have inspired early myths about what legendary creature?

6. The Wren in Cambridge, UK, the Strahov in Prague, Czech Republic, and the Congress in Washington, D.C., are all what type of institution?

7. Who was the father of Isaac?

8. Which English king was known as the Lionheart?

9. Which West African nation achieved independence in 1960 from France?

10. Which Roman general and lover of Cleopatra was defeated by Octavian at the Battle of Actium?

11. What is Microsoft's operating system called?

Ten of the answers in the grid below are the names of famous playwrights. The other five are not. Can you cross out the wrong answers, leaving only the ten dramatists in tact?

O'NEILL	MILLER	STRINDBERG
SHAW	UPDIKE	KEROUAC
CHEKHOV	DICKENS	PLATH
IBSEN	BECKETT	MORRISON
WILDE	WILLIAMS	BRECHT

How many squares can you see in the grid below?

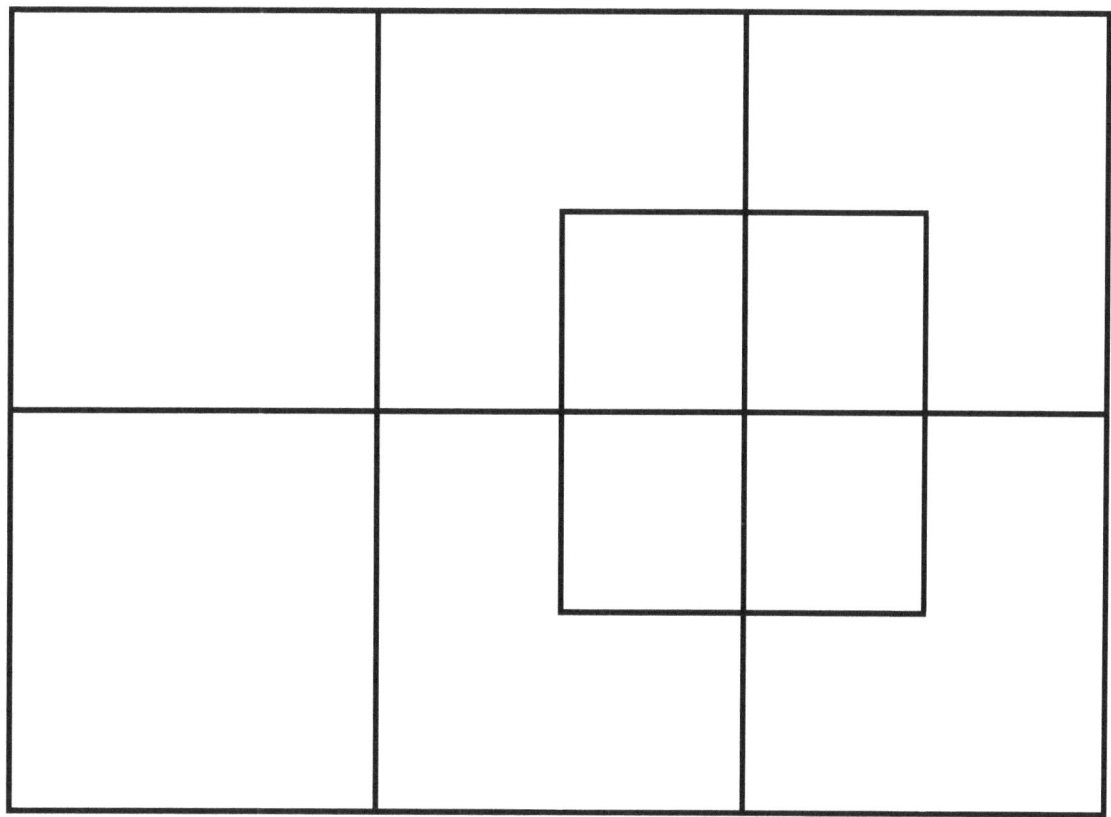

The names of six items of classroom equipment have been jumbled up here.

Can you unscramble each of them?

LOHARDBACK

SACKOBOE

ASRICH

ELITEVINOS

TRUCEMOP

BADCROUP

There are five classes on the timetable today: class 1A, 2B, 3C, 4D, and 5E.

Each class starts on the hour: one at 9am, one at 10am, another at 11am, one at 1pm, and another at 2pm.

Based on the clues below, can you work out at what time each class will have their lesson?

1. Class 3C are not the first class of the day, and class 2B are not the last.

2. The class whose lesson is at 1pm have a number in their name two higher than the class whose lesson is at 9am.

3. Class 1A has their lesson immediately after class 2B.

4. Class 5E do not have their lesson at 11am.

CLASS	TIME
1A	
2B	
3C	
4D	
5E	

How many of these items of school gym equipment can you find in the grid below?

- BALANCE BEAM
- BARBELL
- BARS
- CLIMBING FRAME
- DUMBBELLS
- EXERCISE BIKE
- MATS
- POMMEL
- RINGS
- ROPES
- ROWER
- SPRINGBOARD
- TRAMPOLINE
- TREADMILL
- VAULTING BOX

```
N X D G H L L J I W D G B E R
Q O N X J P L W S U E E A T B
L B S T A M E I M E L M R N M
J G C V X W R B M G P A S A H
T N Q I H O B B P D M O E O S
R I N G S E J H C P A B R Y P
L T F P L R E W O R E E I K R
L L K L O W R L H C Q B R Q I
E U S Y J M I T N G P J L T N
B A A N T N M A C S S X G U G
R V A E E L E J X D N G I B
A O M H J A F L L W K W L F O
B F T K B T A Y G U D A P F A
E X E R C I S E B I K E C K R
E M A R F G N I B M I L C K D
```

Time for a little home economics! Listed on the left here are the names of eight dishes. On the right, are the names of their main ingredient. Can you correctly match all eight pairs together? The first has been filled in for you to make a start.

MERINGUE ☐ ———————————— ☐ Potato

PANNA COTTA ☐ ☐ Beet

GAZPACHO ☐ ☐ Egg white

HASH BROWN ☐ ☐ Rice

COQ AU VIN ☐ ☐ Seafood

CHOWDER ☐ ☐ Tomato

BIBIMBAP ☐ ☐ Chicken

BORSCHT ☐ ☐ Cream

Here's another quick crossword to get stuck into.

Across

1. Condition (5)
4. Removes feeling (5)
10. Nonspecific (7)
11. More protected (5)
12. Pleasant (4)
13. Detached (8)
15. Configuration (11)
19. Alfresco (8)
20. Make a noise like a cat (4)
23. Proof you were elsewhere at the time of a crime (5)
24. Mansions, ranches (7)
25. Fulcrum (5)
26. Church tower (5)

Down

2. Stimulant (5)
3. Ripped (4)
5. Parvenus (8)
6. Bison (7)
7. Professional representative (5)
8. Accoutrements (11)
9. Doctrine (5)
14. Contradictory (8)
16. Summary (7)
17. Sum (5)
18. Unused (5)
21. Put into words (5)
22. Pace (4)

Can you find your way through this maze from one side to the other?

Can you solve this cryptogram to uncover a stereotypical excuse for late homework?

"M_ H_____ _ L A__ E_____

"PV RQWA KMTT QOTMMY QWA

___ _____'_ ____ __ ____ __!"

F AFAW'X LQWX XD LQJM FX!"

40

Something for the math teachers here with this numbercross!

Across

1. 13 x 13
4. 579 - 244
6. 2 DOWN x 5
7. 73 + 77
8. 21 x 25
9. 2,10,405 x 5
13. 3,755 x 15
17. 263 x 3
18. 30 x 16
19. 550 x 80
20. 234 * 3
21. 41 x 3

Down

1. 101 x 12
2. 1,881 x 5
3. 20 x 20 x 10
4. 711 x 5
5. 10,000 − 4,844
10. 16 squared
11. 555 − 333
12. 3030 x 9
13. 2,284 + 3,658
14. 50 x 60
15. 2672 + 2729
16. 685 + 358

Complete this classic sudoku grid by filling in the numbers 1–9 so that each row, each column, and each smaller set of 3 x 3 squares contain each number just once and once only.

	7	6	4					
		9	5	6	8		1	
						9		
			8	4		6		
6				3		4	9	
				9	7	5	2	
7			9	8			3	6
	6			2	4			
9	1	2	3			8		7

> ### DID YOU KNOW
>
> Since the 1950s, there has been a 96% increase in the number of students in the USA—but a 252% increase in the number of teachers!

The Teaching Calendar:

JANUARY	FEBRUARY	MARCH
APRIL	**MAY**	**JUNE**
JULY	**AUGUST**	**SEPTEMBER**
OCTOBER	**NOVEMBER**	**DECEMBER**

Being a science teacher means a lot more than being well versed in biology, chemistry, and physics. As well as those three, can you find the right homes for all 15 of these branches of high school science in the grid below?

- ANATOMY
- ANTHROPOLOGY
- ASTRONOMY
- BIOLOGY
- BOTANY
- CHEMISTRY
- COSMOLOGY
- ECOLOGY
- ENGINEERING
- GRAVITY
- IMMUNOLOGY
- LOGIC
- MEDICINE
- MICROBIOLOGY
- PHYSICS
- ZOOLOGY

In this acrostic puzzle, place the answers to the trivia questions into the corresponding rows in the grid below, and the name of a high school punishment will be spelled out down the shaded column.

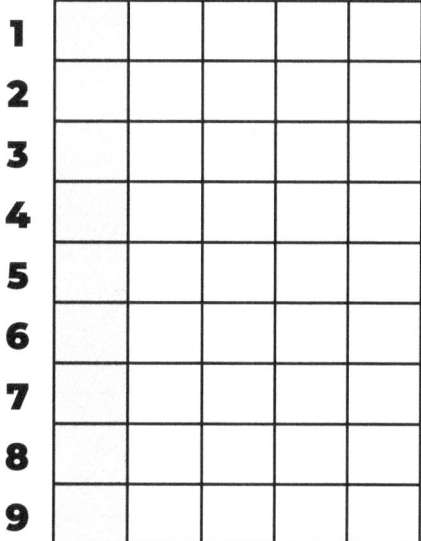

1. An LED is a light emitting what?
2. In what country is the only surviving Wonder of the Ancient World located?
3. Who was the ibis-headed god of the Moon in Egyptian mythology?
4. A two-headed form of what bird features on the flag of Albania?
5. Who is Bill Sykes' lover in Dickens' Oliver Twist?
6. What is the tenth month of the Hebrew calendar?
7. What precious white material is made from the polished dentine of elephants' tusks?
8. Located between Utah and Gold, what was the second most westerly of the five D-Day beaches used by Allied troops in the Normandy Landings?
9. Who was 37th President of the United States?

Here's a tricky picture puzzle for you.

Are there more A+ grades, A grades, or A- grades in the grid below?

      A+   A   A-

A+	A	A-	A+	A	A+	A-	A
A-	A	A-	A	A+	A-	A+	A
A	A+	A-	A+	A-	A+	A	A+
A	A+	A	A+	A-	A	A	A+
A+	A-	A+	A	A+	A-	A+	A-
A+	A+	A-	A-	A	A+	A-	A
A+	A-	A-	A+	A+	A	A	A-

Can you find your way through this maze from one side to the other?

47

Did you know there are 10 million high school students studying a foreign language in the US school system alone? And of those, 93% are studying Spanish! How many of these languages can you find in the grid below?

- DUTCH
- ENGLISH
- FRENCH
- GERMAN
- ITALIAN
- JAPANESE
- LATIN
- MANDARIN
- NAVAJO
- NORWEGIAN
- OJIBWE
- PORTUGUESE
- RUSSIAN
- SPANISH
- TURKISH

```
O N O E B C M E N Z D V K A Y
J I Y W A D S A N A V A J O N
I T U U Z E O Q O P I U E A S
B A H R N F W X F O X L I G R
W L Q A R K O K L R F S A Y F
E L P E T P T E L T S B V T T
M A N D A R I N N U L N A B I
J C S A Z I Q L R G F N R R G
H S X H I E J N V U L E D E H
O J C R A G B Z P E C I R U S
H C T U D K E B N S P M S N I
H S I N A P S W P E A X I H K
X M N T B D P H R N Y R V G R
K W O P I R N Q G O L L U B U
E M F M X U D Q E Y N C N T T
```

Here's another tricky test from citizenship class. On each of the lines below, the names of two US presidents have been jumbled together. Can you unjumble each pair? The first has been done for you to make a start.

1. **ADEEFKNNTTY**

   KENNEDY and TAFT

2. **ACGHIILLNNNNOOSTW**

3. **AABEHMOOORV**

4. **AAADDGHIMNRS**

5. **AEHILNORRRSTY**

6. **CDEEEGILLOOOORSTV**

7. **AABCEJKNNNORSUV**

8. **ACDEEHJLLNNNOOSV**

How's your knowledge of the world? Ten of the answers in the grid below are the names of EU member countries in which the euro is the main unit of currency.

The other five are not. Can you cross out the wrong answers, leaving only the ten correct Eurozone nations intact?

BULGARIA	LUXEMBOURG	CYPRUS
ESTONIA	RUSSIA	POLAND
IRELAND	AUSTRIA	CROATIA
BELGIUM	SLOVENIA	FINLAND
NORWAY	SLOVAKIA	SWITZERLAND

Here's a fiendish test of your anatomical knowledge. As any good biology teacher will no doubt tell you, the names of 14 bones in the human body are hidden in the grid below. Unlike in an ordinary word search, though, they're not written in a straight line! Can you find all the answers, so that no letter is left over, and no letter is used more than once? The first has been filled in for you to make a start.

C	L	A	A	T	L	A	E	T	A
E	T	V	P	E	L	M	M	A	T
R	S	I	C	L	E	A	S	R	F
N	S	U	M	U	H	N	A	R	E
U	S	R	E	B	I	D	L	U	M
M	C	E	M	L	T	I	B	I	A
P	A	T	A	E	C	A	L	U	I
U	H	A	C	F	I	A	C	S	D
L	Y	R	P	A	B	N	E	U	A
A	O	I	D	L	U	L	A	S	R

51

Empty out your pencil case—can you find homes for all fifteen of these items of stationery in the grid below?

- CLIP
- COMPASS
- ERASER
- FASTENERS
- FOLDER
- GLUESTICK
- NOTEBOOK
- PAPER
- PEN
- PENCIL
- PROTRACTOR
- SCISSORS
- SHARPENER
- STAMP
- STAPLER

Here's a tricky play on a sudoku game. Can you fill in the timetable below so that no subject—ART, DRAMA, MUSIC, MATH, HISTORY, and GYM—appears more than once in each row, each column, and each set of six smaller squares?

	Music	Drama		Math	Art
History			Gym		Drama
Drama	Math	Art			
		Gym		Art	Math
			Art		
	Drama	Music	Math	History	Gym

Can you solve this cryptogram to uncover a stereotypical excuse for late homework?

" _ _ I _ D _ O _ _ _ _ E

"V SVSZ'N SX VN PQBCRMQ

_ _ _ _ _ _ ' _ T _ _ A _

V SVSZ'N OCZN NX CSS

_ _ _ _ _ _ W _ _ _ _ _ _ !"

NX AXRD OXDWJXCS!"

55

Can you find your way through this maze from one side to the other?

Complete this classic sudoku grid by filling in the numbers 1–9 so that each row, each column, and each smaller set of 3 x 3 squares contain each number just once and once only.

1	5		9	7			3	
8		4			5	9		7
	3	9	4	8		6	5	
5	4			1			8	
								5
	8	7	3	5	9			
3				9	4			
9	7							8
4	2		1	6				3

> ### ✦ DID YOU KNOW ✦
>
> **9 out of 10 teachers in the US admit to spending their own money on things for their students, or for equipment for their classroom**

Place the answers to the trivia questions into the corresponding rows in the grid below, and the name of a school subject will be spelled out down the shaded column.

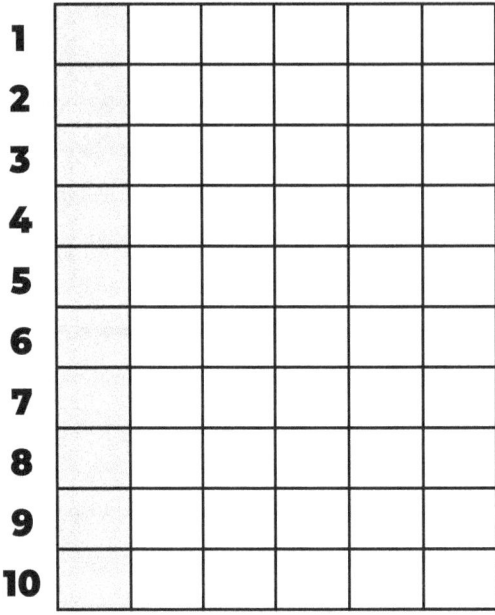

1. In economics, what is defined as excess of revenues over outlays?

2. The African republic of Chad is almost entirely covered by what desert?

3. What Japanese multinational manufacturer of motor vehicles and musical instruments was founded in 1955?

4. Who was the leader of the centaurs in Greek legend?

5. Who (surname only) served as attorney general of California from 2011–17, and as US senator for California from 2017–21?

6. Who was the brother of Set in Egyptian mythology?

7. Hammersmith is an area of what European capital?

8. In what city is the world's oldest university located?

9. What is the southernmost country on Europe's Balkan peninsula?

10. Goldenrod is a shade of what primary color?

Six teachers—Mr. Phips, Miss Quigley, Mrs. Robinson, Ms. Simmonds, Mr. Thomson, and Mr. Underwood—have put their lunch in the staff room fridge. Someone has brought a cheese sandwich; someone has leftover lasagna; someone has a ham quiche; someone has some tomato soup; another has a chicken salad; and someone else has some mac and cheese.

Based on the clues below, can you work out who is having what for lunch?

1. The name of the teacher who is having lasagna does not have an N in it.

2. The teacher who is having mac and cheese is a woman, and the teacher who is having a cheese sandwich is a man.

3. The surname of the teacher who has brought the ham quiche in for their lunch is listed alphabetically immediately after the teacher having the lasagna, and immediately before the teacher having the mac and cheese.

4. Mr. Underwood is a vegetarian.

5. Mr. Phips is not having pasta of any kind, and Mr. Thomson is not having soup.

TEACHER	LUNCH
Mr. Phips	
Miss Quigley	
Mrs. Robinson	
Ms. Simmonds	
Mr. Thomson	
Mr. Underwood	

This word search is all about the rooms in a high school. How many of these can you find in the grid below?

ARTROOM	**GYMNASIUM**	**RECEPTION**
CHANGING ROOMS	**LIBRARY**	**SCIENCE LAB**
CLASSROOM	**LOCKERS**	**STAFF ROOM**
DETENTION	**MUSIC ROOM**	**STUDY ROOM**
DINING HALL	**PRINCIPAL'S / OFFICE**	**THEATER**

```
L L A H G N I N I D M N L K S
S L A P I C N I R P O M K R M
D C V C N G K J V P O P E D O
N O I T P E C E R P R K L E O
R M F E O M Y K S M C G I T R
E N H D N N U T M O I D B E S
T L G R P C A I L F S A R N S
A N M U R F E I S E U H A T A
E B E A F N H L I A M H R I L
H A H R U C W W A Y N E Y O C
T X O E H C D L F B O M F N P
M O O R Y D U T S N B F Y A F
M G I L Q A R T R O O M J G S
C H A N G I N G R O O M S E V
K Q T X D N F E C I F F O X L
```

Time for a bit of homework from English class. Listed on the left here are the names of eight Shakespearean characters. On the right, are the plays in which they appear. Can you correctly match all eight together? The first has been filled in for you to make a start.

BANQUO ☐	☐ Julius Caesar
OBERON ☐	☐ The Tempest
VIOLA ☐	☐ Macbeth
BRUTUS ☐	☐ Hamlet
CORDELIA ☐	☐ The Taming of the Shrew
PROSPERO ☐	☐ Twelfth Night
KATHERINE ☐	☐ King Lear
OPHELIA ☐	☐ A Midsummer Night's Dream

(Banquo → Macbeth)

Time for another quick crossword to get stuck into!

Across

1. Location (5)
4. Hurts with a knife (5)
10. Biggest (7)
11. In the countryside (5)
12. Utters (4)
13. Weather report (8)
15. Subterranean (11)
19. Arms (8)
20. Cab (4)
23. Part (5)
24. Teach (7)
25. Hoard (5)
26. Touches the surface only (5)

Down

1. Truck (5)
3. Cook (4)
5. Underwater projectiles (8)
6. Cheap deal (7)
7. Cut (5)
8. Forced (11)
9. Dish (5)
14. Returns to good health (8)
16. Most proximate (7)
17. Used a brush (5)
18. Dwells (5)
21. Morning wakeup call (5)
22. Elephant's tooth (4)

Let's take a turn in the science lab. Ten of the answers in the grid below are the names of chemical elements. The other five are not. Can you cross out the wrong answers, leaving only the ten entries from the periodic table in place?

CARBON	ASTATINE	BORON
BROMIDE	MANGANESE	CYANIDE
ARSENIC	ZINC	PROTON
ZIRCON	IODINE	TUNGSTEN
BRONZE	TIN	IRON

How many squares can you count in the shape below?

Can you unjumble the school lunch menu below?

Today's Menu

- HAREM GRUB
- CHASED MENACE
- TIGHT PEAS
- PINK COUCHES
- ACHED EASELS

Can you find your way through this maze from one side to the other?

Can you solve this cryptogram to uncover this pupil's ridiculous excuse for their late homework?

"MY CAT ATE IT, KNOWING THAT I'D
"FZ GXR XRH JR, KVQTJVC RMXR J'L

BLAME THE DOG INSTEAD."
DEXFH RMH LQC JVNRHXL."

We're in library for this puzzle. Can you unjumble the titles of these classic books?

Starting at the X in the top left corner here, complete all the squares in the grid below using each of the calculations between them to fill in the gaps.

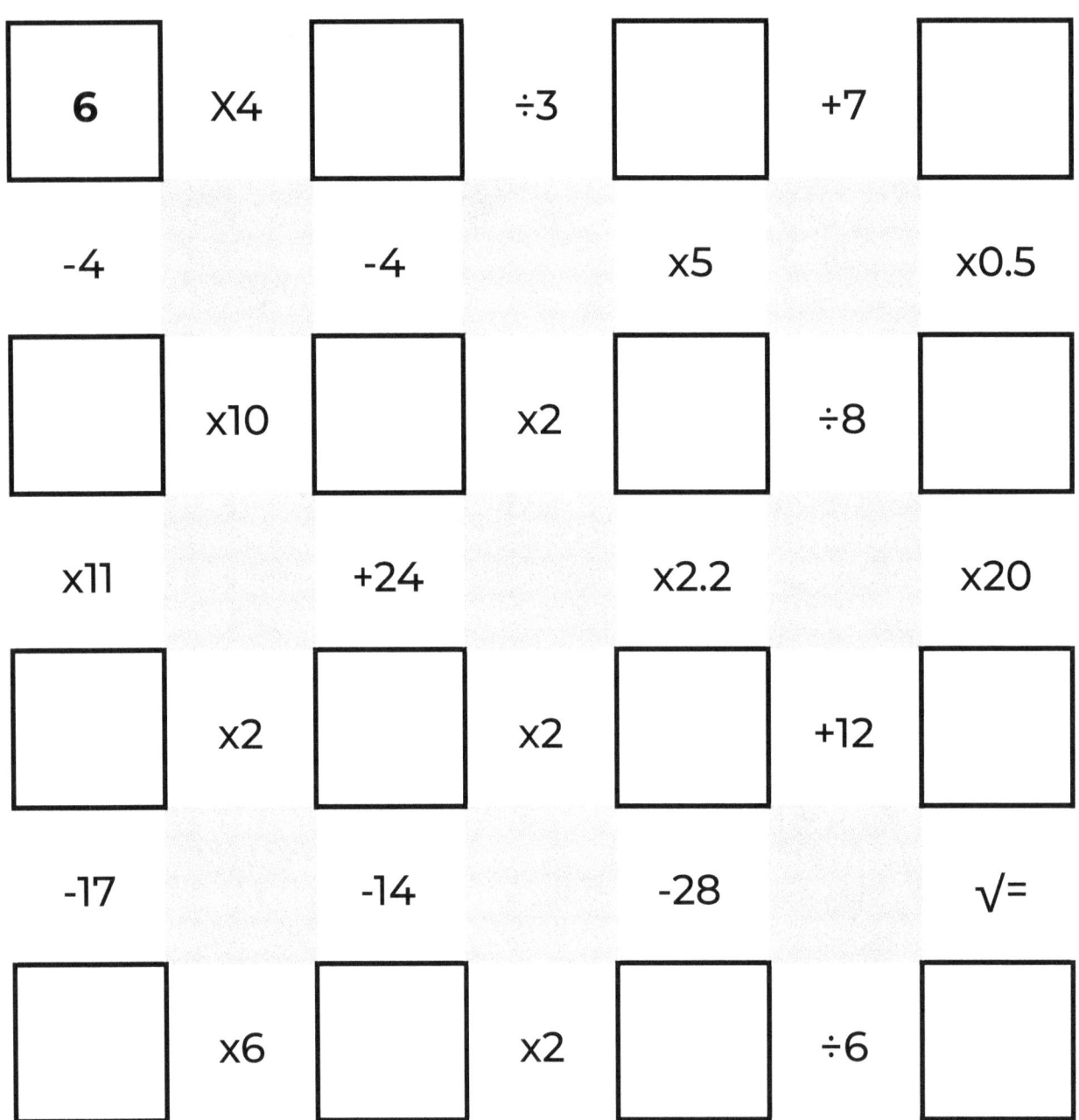

TEACHERS DECIPHERING THEIR KIDS' HANDWRITING:

Complete this classic sudoku grid by filling in the numbers 1–9 so that each row, each column, and each smaller set of 3 x 3 squares contain each number just once and once only.

6		2	8		9		5	
3				6	7		8	9
4								7
8	2		1			5	3	
1			7	2		8		
5	6			8		2	7	
				1	3	7	6	5
	5	1		7	2	3		
	3				8			

DID YOU KNOW

Phuma Changthang, a town in Tibet, is said to be the site of the world's highest school. Located among the Himalayas, it's 5373m (17,600ft) above sea level!

The school drama department are handing out the roles for their next production—a revival of the musical, Oliver! Six students—Jamie, Kenny, Linda, Marina, Owen, and Philip—are reading the playbill announcement to find out who is playing who: someone has been cast in the title role; someone is playing Fagin; another is playing the Artful Dodger; someone is playing Bill Sykes; someone is playing Nancy; and someone has only been cast in the chorus, as one of Fagin's boys.

Based only on the clues below, can you figure out who has been cast in which role?

1. The name of the boy who has been cast as the Artful Dodger is listed alphabetically immediately after the name of the boy who has been cast as Fagin.

2. The drama teacher was so impressed by her audition that the title role of Oliver has been given to one of the girls!

3. Owen has not been cast as Fagin, and Kenny has not been cast in the chorus.

4. Nancy and Bill Sykes are being played by a girl and a boy whose names are the same length.

STUDENT	ROLE
Jamie	
Kenny	
Linda	
Marina	
Owen	
Philip	

Did you hear the one about the student who said he'd do his homework tomorrow because he'll be ... what? Place the answers to the questions into the corresponding rows in the grid below, to spell out the rest of the excuse down the shaded column!

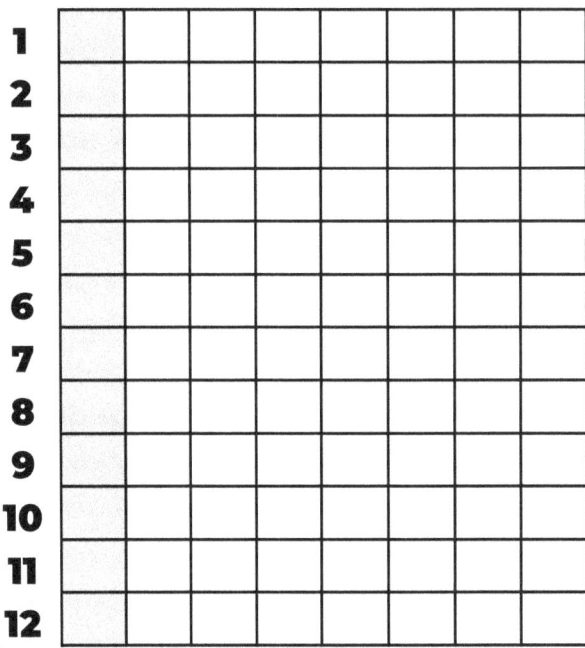

1. What nationality is the authoress Margaret Atwood?
2. In fashion, what word for women's undergarments derives from the French word for linen?
3. What was the nickname of the US B-29 bomber that in 1945 became the first aircraft to drop an atomic bomb in warfare? (5, 3)
4. In what US state did the London Company establish the first permanent English colony in the New World in 1607?
5. Addis Ababa is the capital of what landlocked African nation?
6. What root vegetable is known as a swede in British English?
7. Who is the lover of Orpheus in Greek mythology?
8. In Russian history, which monk and mystic was infamously the court advisor of Tsar Nicholas II?
9. Which English poet wrote *The Lady of Shalott*, and *Break, Break, Break*?
10. Who (surname only) was elected 9th president of the US in 1841?
11. What name completes the traditional Christmas carol, O Come, O Come, _____ ?
12. What gas has the chemical symbol N?

Let's head back down the science lab for this one. Listed on the left here are the names of nine sciences. On the right, are the subjects of those nine fields of study. Can you correctly match the pairs together? The first has been filled in for you to make a start...

BOTANY ☐		☐ Fungi
MYCOLOGY ☐		☐ Sound
OPTICS ☐		☐ Earthquakes
ASTRONOMY ☐		☐ Plants
SEISMOLOGY ☐		☐ Fossils
GLACIOLOGY ☐		☐ Light
PALEONTOLOGY ☐		☐ Ice
ACOUSTICS ☐		☐ Space
HYDROLOGY ☐		☐ Water

Here's one for the math teachers! Ten of the three-digit answers in the grid below are square numbers. The other five are not. Can you cross out the wrong answers, leaving only the ten correct squares—quite literally!—in place?

225	466	289
156	169	196
633	961	472
256	505	900
100	676	441

This puzzle is all about high school sports. How many of these sports and games can you find in the grid?

- ARCHERY
- ATHLETICS
- FOOTBALL
- GYMNASTICS
- HOCKEY
- LACROSSE
- NETBALL
- RUGBY
- SOCCER
- SOFTBALL
- SWIMMING
- TENNIS
- TRACK
- VOLLEYBALL
- WRESTLING

```
L L A B T O O F R L P I T B L
T E R R A S T G L E S Z B Z L
D V A G R K Q A H O C K E Y A
L C O M C R B X N O Y C J O B
K U C K H Y W T B Q O B O D T
X E X R E M D R T W M R G S E
C S P L R T U S E C X A C U N
Z S L U Y C E X R S D I P A R
L O J S C I T E L H T A G T E
V R T L U I D K U S H L U J F
D C U E J N R K A Y M D I B G
E A K G N X U N S L S Y G N A
F L F W G N M S W I M M I N G
D Y T K B Y I L L A B T F O S
P D X A G Y S S R Q H R E Q H
```

Here's another tricky picture puzzle for you.

Are there more pens, pencils, or artist's brushes in the grid below?

PEN   PENCIL   BRUSH

In this mini crossword, all the answers are anagrams of the clues. Watch out, though—if there's more than one possible answer, you'll have to work out which one is correct!

Across

1. PURES
2. POCHE
7. ANIMA
8. GRADE
9. DECAL
12. ENDOW
13. SLEEK
14. YELTS.

Down

1. MESA
2. CANDLEPIN
3. RARE
4. CANOPYING
5. DOSH
9. KALE
10. SODS
11. GEED

Two five-letter words that mean opposite things have been jumbled together here. What are they?

A A E G
L L L M R S

Can you find your way through this maze from one side to the other?

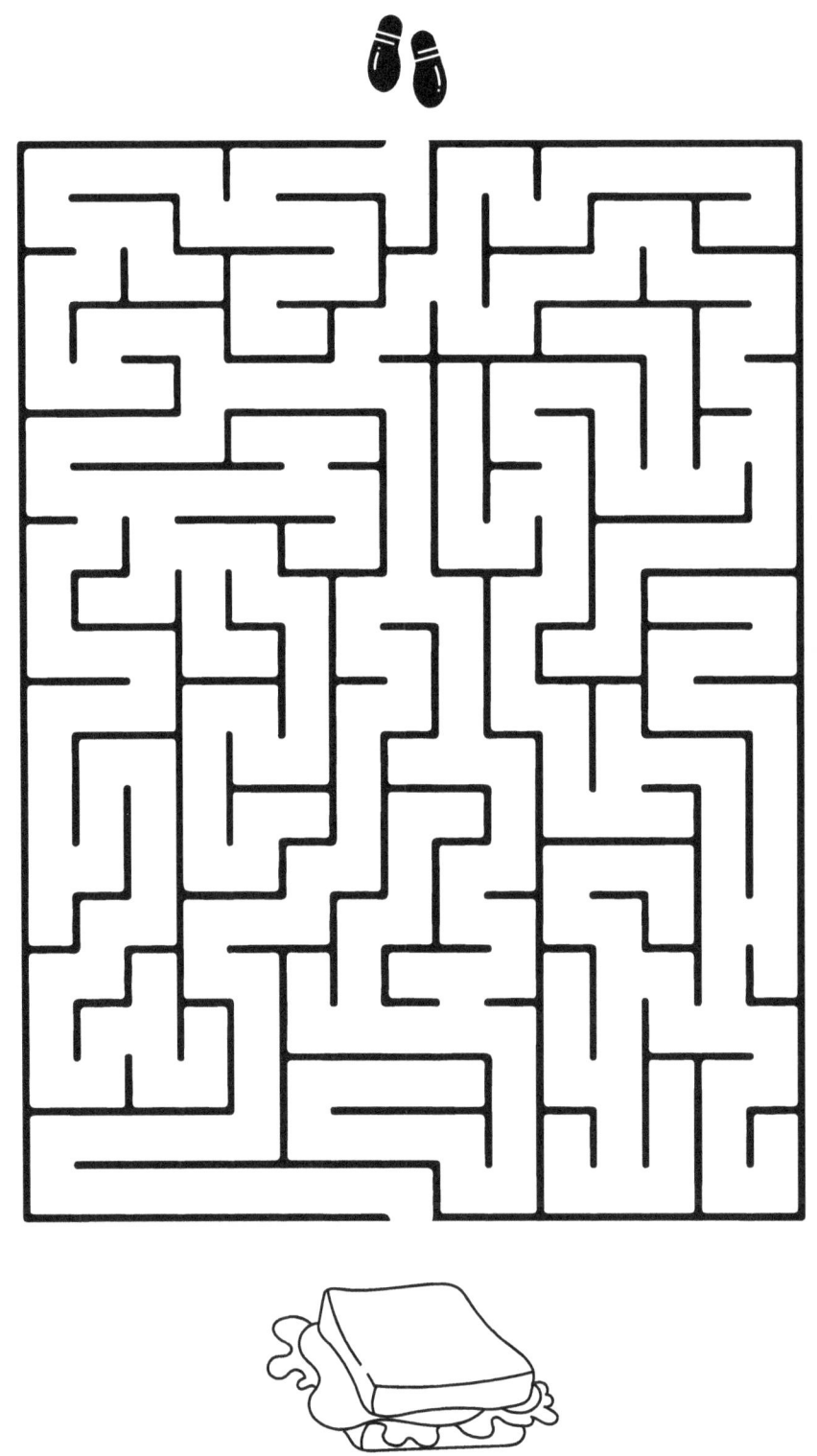

We're off to the school library for this one! All the things you might find in a library listed here link together in the grid. Can you find the right home for each one?

BOOKS
CATALOG
COMPUTERS
DESKS
DEWEY DECIMAL
GLOBE
INKPAD
LIBRARIAN
MICROFICHE
MOVIES
OFFICE
PENS
PERIODICALS
PHOTOCOPIER
PINBOARDS
READING ROOMS
SHELVES
STAMP

Start the timer—here's another quick crossword to get your brain around!

Across

1. Female sibling (6)
7. Positioned (6)
8. Grownups (6)
9. For this reason (7)
10. Child (6)
11. High-ranking card (3)
13. In that place (5)
16. Plead (3)
19. Cleans with water vapor (6)
20. Musical performance (7)
21. Spicy sausage (6)
22. Animal seen on 5 DOWN (7)
23. Powerful (6)

Down

1. Endurance (7)
2. Edge, move slightly (7)
3. No longer living (7)
4. Eternally (7)
5. African wildlife trek (6)
6. Missive (7)
12. Of a disease, long-lasting (7)
14. Scare (7)
15. Excerpt (7)
16. Boldness (7)
17. Panting for breath (7)
18. Outgoing (6)

Complete this classic sudoku grid by filling in the numbers 1–9 so that each row, each column, and each smaller set of 3 x 3 squares contain each number just once and once only.

1	6							2
7		4	1	8	3		5	
5						3	4	1
			6	4	8		1	
	1			9	7		3	
			3				7	
	5			2				7
				6		8	2	4
			7		4			3

> **DID YOU KNOW**
>
> In French schools, meal time is considered an inherent part of the national curriculum, and is used to encourage pupils to learn about food!

Six schoolchildren—David, Erica, Fabien, Georgia, Harrison, and India—are each giving a presentation in class today. Each one has picked their favorite subject to talk about: someone is talking about science fiction; someone is talking about reading; another is talking about bird watching; someone is talking about fishing; another is talking about ballet; and someone else is talking about baseball.

Based on the clues below, can you figure out which pupil is talking about what?

1. The students who go fishing and bird watching at the weekends both have names ending in vowels.

2. The boy who is talking about reading their favorite books has a 5-letter name...

3. ...as does the girl who is talking about her favorite sci-fi movies.

4. Harrison is a baseball fanatic, but Erica doesn't like sci-fi, and Georgia definitely isn't talking about fishing!

PUPIL	TOPIC
David	
Erica	
Fabien	
Georgia	
Harrison	
India	

Place the answers to the trivia questions into the corresponding rows in the grid below, and the name of something from a school bag will be spelled out down the shaded column.

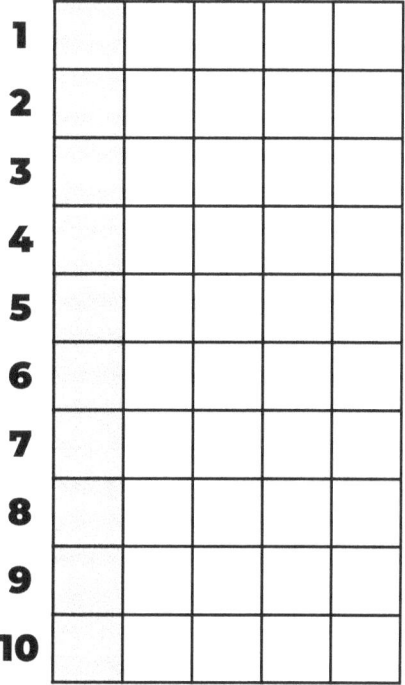

1. Despite being known as a bear, what black and white mammal was once thought to be more closely related to the racoon?
2. How many players are there in an octet?
3. Mount Everest straddles the border between China and what other Asian nation?
4. What is the Latin word for dog?
5. In what European country are the ruins of Pompeii?
6. What is the largest island in the Philippines called?
7. In what game might a pawn be promoted for reaching the opposite side of the board?
8. In Greek mythology, who was punished by being made to hold up the heavens on his shoulders?
9. How many sides does a heptagon have?
10. What black wood was once traditionally used to make the sharp and flat keys on a piano?

Jumbled together on each line here are two terms from a different high school subject. Can you unjumble the pairs? The first has been solved for you to make a start...

Math:

Algebra (7) 1. AAABEEGILNOQRTU Equation (8)

Drama:

_____ (9) 2. AACEEHILPRRRSST _____ (6)

Physics:

_____ (4) 3. ACEELMNOORTT _____ (8)

Geography:

_____ (5) 4. AAACEILLMSTT _____ (7)

English:

_____ (7) 5. AAEGMMOPRRRS _____ (5)

Biology:

_____ (4) 6. ABCEEELLMMNR _____ (8)

Art:

(8) 7. ACEILOPPRRRSTTTUU _____ (9)

Chemistry:

_____ (6) 8. AAEEEIKLLLMNT _____ (7)

Time for history class! Ten of the answers in the grid below are famous historical figures who were alive in the 1900s. The other five were not. Can you cross out the wrong answers, leaving only the ten correct 20th century figures intact?

NAPOLEON	EDWARD VIII	SITTING BULL
MOTHER THERESA	ALBERT EINSTEIN	MAHATMA GANDHI
ROBERT FALCON SCOTT	DAVID LIVINGSTONE	WINSTON CHURCHILL
LIZZIE BORDEN	PABLO PICASSO	VINCENT VAN GOGH
ZACHARY TAYLOR	EMMELINE PANKHURST	JOHN DILLINGER

The names of 14 famous poets are hidden in the grid below. Unlike in an ordinary word search though, they're not written in a straight line! Can you find all the answers, so that no letter is left over, and no letter is used more than once? The first has been filled in for you to make a start.

W	H	I	Y	E	A	T	N	O	T
I	D	T	O	R	F	S	L	P	L
C	A	M	S	T	G	N	I	I	I
K	N	O	N	E	M	E	R	K	M
I	Y	R	S	Y	N	O	S	E	G
N	B	H	O	N	D	O	N	N	N
S	O	T	N	N	Y	B	R	N	I
H	N	A	L	E	E	W	O	W	H
U	E	S	P	T	L	O	S	W	T
G	H	S	H	E	L	R	D	O	R

Time for a good old high school show! How many of these drama department terms can you find in the grid below before curtain up?

CASTING
COSTUMES
CURTAINCALL
IMPROV
LEAD ROLE
LINES
MUSICAL
ORCHESTRA
PERFORMANCE
PREMIERE
PROGRAM
PROMPT
PROPS
REHEARSALS
UNDERSTUDY

```
X Q J Y I S H G R I S N B H S
S J Y T M P L O A P E K N C E
M Z D F P R B A O W A X P P M
X W U O R E H R S K M H L L U
H C T T O M P F I R C O E E T
C C S Z V I B P A U A A H B S
P A R T S E H C R O D E Z O O
R S E Z L R M T N R H I H S C
O M D X U E A X O A W D M E Y
G H N F D I P L A C I S U M R
R L U P N C E R E Y S N P H V
A L P C P E R F O R M A N C E
M U A L I N E S C M F K H A Q
A L G N I T S A C X P B K D P
L U R N O P Q V N M B T R L X
```

Starting at the X in the top left corner here, complete all the squares in the grid below using each of the calculations between them to fill in the gaps.

7	+3		x3.5		+5	
x7		x4		÷7		÷2
	-9		÷8		x4	
+6		+9		x6		+1
	-6		-19		-9	
÷6		√=		-11		÷7
	-2		+12		-16	

92

Can you find your way through this maze from one side to the other?

"PETITION TO REPLACE THE PHRASE 'RABBIT IN THE HEADLIGHTS' WITH 'TEACHER ON THEIR FIRST DAY.'"

Here's another tricky picture puzzle for you.

Are there more left-handed or right-handed students in the grid below?

LEFT-HANDED   RIGHT-HANDED

Listed on the left here are the names of the eight planets in our solar system. On the right, are their numerical rank, in order 1st to 8th. Can you correctly match all eight pairs together? The first has been filled in for you to make a start.

MERCURY	☐————————————☐	1st
EARTH	☐ ☐	2nd
SATURN	☐ ☐	3rd
NEPTUNE	☐ ☐	4th
JUPITER	☐ ☐	5th
VENUS	☐ ☐	6th
URANUS	☐ ☐	7th
MARS	☐ ☐	8th

We're taking one last trip to the science lab for this crisscross puzzle. The 18 words and phrases from the water cycle below connect together in the grid. Can you find the right home for each one?

AQUIFER	INFILTRATION	RUNOFF
CONDENSATION	LAKE	SEA
EROSION	PERCOLATION	SNOW
EVAPORATION	PRECIPITATION	SNOWMELT
FOG	RAIN	TRANSPIRATION
GROUNDWATER	RIVER	WATERTABLE

Complete this classic sudoku grid by filling in the numbers 1–9 so that each row, each column, and each smaller set of 3 x 3 squares contain each number just once and once only.

		8			1	7		3
6	7		3	2			4	
		1	7					2
3	2					5	6	
5		6				8	7	
9	8	4			7	3	2	1
1	9	2		7			5	6
8	4		9				3	
7			4			9		

DID YOU KNOW

According to a worldwide UNESCO survey of schools around the globe, girls are less likely to attend school than boys—but boys are more likely to have to repeat grades.

There are seven pupils left to be picked up by the school bus: Alice, Beatrice, Christopher, Daniel, Edgar, Fred, and Greta. Each one lives on a different block: Main Street, High Street, Front Street, West Road, North Road, South Avenue, and East Avenue.

Based on the clues below, can you work out who lives where?

1. The name of the pupil who lives on North Road comes alphabetically immediately before the pupil who lives on Front Street, and alphabetically two places before the pupil who lives on East Avenue.

2. Beatrice does not live on South Avenue...

3. ...and Christopher does not live on Main Street!

4. One of the pupils shares the first two letters of their name with the first two letters of their address.

5. The three girls all live at addresses with compass points in their names.

PUPIL	ADDRESS
Alice	
Beatrice	
Christopher	
Daniel	
Edgar	
Fred	
Greta	

Things are getting a little tougher in this acrostic puzzle! Place the 13-letter answers to the 10 trivia questions into the corresponding rows in the grid below, and the name of something you might find in a geography classroom will be spelled out down the shaded column.

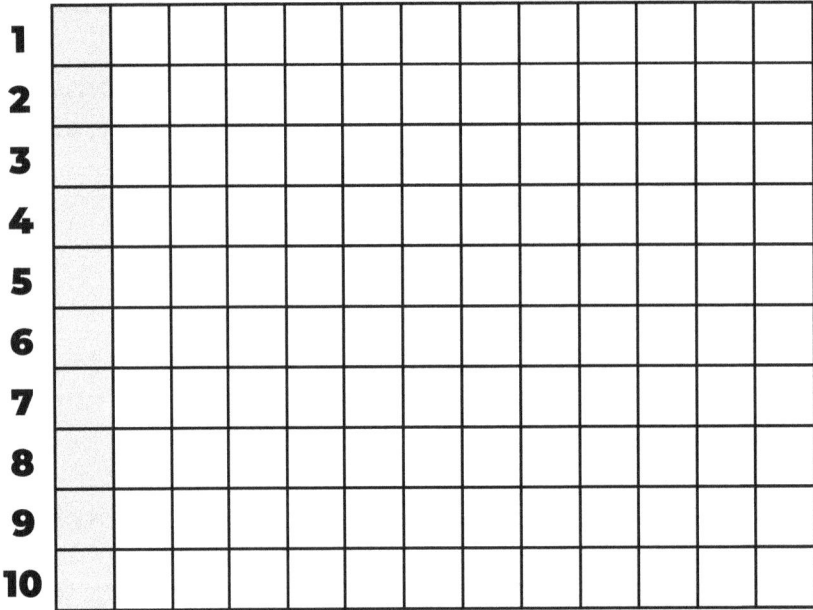

1. Which famous Elizabethan English statesman and explorer was executed in London in 1618? (6,7)
2. What great superpower existed in southwest Europe and eastern Asia from the 1200s until the mid-20th century? (7,6)
3. Which 17th century mathematician and philosopher introduced the coordinates as a means of locating points in two and three dimensions? (4,9)
4. What tiny European principality is located between Switzerland and Austria?
5. What name is given to the national holiday celebrated in the US on the last Monday in May? (10,3)
6. What is the second nearest star to Earth, after the Sun? (5,8)
7. In the Christian calendar, what is the eighth Sunday after Easter known as? (7,6)
8. What 1862 novel by Victor Hugo features the character Jean Valjean? (3,10)
9. The Sargasso Sea is the only sea on Earth that is not surrounded by land. What larger body of water is it instead entirely surrounded by? (8,5)
10. Who wrote Waiting for Godot? (6,7)

In this word jumble crossword, each of the answers is an anagram of the clue word. Watch out, though—if there's more than one possible answer, you'll have to work out which one is correct!

Across

1. OWL
2. RIA
6. SHALL
7. HES
8. CHI
9. ELWYN
13. BEAMY
17. OPE
18. TEN
19. AIDER
20. ANT
21. ADS

Down

1. SOLE
2. HEWN
3. WOLF
4. SHAY
5. CARE
10. ARE
11. ALB
12. TOPS
13. NAME
14. DRAY
15. SEND
16. DUST

Can you solve this cryptogram to uncover a stereotypical excuse for late homework?

"_ _ T _ _ _ _ N' W _ _ _ I _ D _ _ _ _ .

"P VPV PD RWD P VPVA'D EUPDG PD VQEA.

_ _ _ ' L _ _ _ _ _ H _ _ _ _ !"

PD'H NMM PA CX BGNV!"

103

How about a classic quick crossword to keep you busy?

Across

1. Snatched (7)
5. Inexpensive (5)
8. Stop from happening (7)
9. Change (5)
10. Room (5)
11. Elucidate (7)
12. Gives money back to (6)
14. Divisions of the year (6)
17. Move up at work (7)
19. Upper leg (5)
22. Bird's sleeping place (5)
23. Versus (7)
24. Pilot a car (5)
25. Organic (7)

Down

1. Opens the mouth (5)
2. Stadium (5)
3. Beer-making factory (7)
4. Spotty (6)
5. Painful muscle contraction (5)
6. Competitor (7)
7. Mothers and fathers (7)
12. School write-ups (7)
13. Suggest (7)
15. One who is shunned (7)
16. Marine (anag., 6)
18. Water-dwelling mammal (5)
20. Internal (5)
21. Guesthouse (5)

Here's one last match game to test your US citizenship knowledge!

Listed on the left here are the names of eight US cities that are not their state capitals, despite being larger than them! On the right, are not the eight states in which they are located, but the state capitals that they are larger than. Can you get your brain around the missing connections to correctly match all eight pairs together? The first has been filled in for you to make a start!

BIRMINGHAM ☐	☐	Dover
JACKSONVILLE ☐	☐	Lincoln
WILMINGTON ☐	☐	Montgomery
ANCHORAGE ☐	☐	Madison
OMAHA ☐	☐	Juneau
MILWAUKEE ☐	☐	Tallahassee
PORTLAND ☐	☐	Bismarck
FARGO ☐	☐	Salem

(Birmingham connected to Montgomery)

Can you find your way through this maze from one side to the other?

Ten of the answers in the grid below are units of length or distance. The other five are certainly still units of measurement—but *not* units used to measure length. Can you cross out the wrong answers, leaving only the ten correct distance markers in place?

KELVIN	LEAGUE	MILE
LIGHT YEAR	PICOSECOND	FURLONG
BUSHEL	CHAIN	CABLE
YARD	QUART	PARSEC
ANGSTROM	PECK	DECAMETER

One last trip down the drama department here! The names of 13 Shakespearean characters are hidden in the grid below. Unlike in an ordinary word search though, they're not written in a straight line! Can you find all the answers, so that no letter is left over, and no letter is used more than once? The first has been filled in for you to make a start.

M	A	C	C	O	R	I	O	L	A
C	Y	D	U	F	I	L	O	U	N
B	M	M	A	F	V	I	S	S	T
E	O	V	L	L	A	A	U	T	I
L	L	I	O	Y	D	C	A	L	I
I	N	E	T	M	M	E	R	C	B
K	H	A	Y	A	C	I	A	U	A
C	E	I	B	T	B	A	G	T	N
O	R	M	A	L	E	I	O	I	O
L	Y	H	S	H	T	T	R	O	P

We're in the science lab for this final word search. How many of these items of chemistry equipment can you find in the grid below?

- BEAKER
- BUNSEN / BURNER
- BURETTE
- CONICAL FLASK
- DROPPER
- FUME HOOD
- GAS TAP
- LIGHTER
- LITMUS PAPER
- MICROSCOPE
- PIPETTE
- TEST TUBE
- THERMOMETER
- TONGS
- VIALS

```
Y Z R C S Z T B G N X W K C R
I L L F O O B A E S E E U E L
U I O N N N S S C A V S T U R
P G Y G Q T I H L L K E N E P
E H S G A R H C Y A M E P U U
T T G P O V R P A O I A R G B
T E S T T U B E M L P V L X K
E R F Q J N G R T S F K J P A
R D U J K J E N U G O L Y W I
U L M R O H O M U U Z E A V F
B A E E T N T O O P B E V S B
B H H N F I R E P P O R D Y K
E Y O R L E P O C S O R C I M
X T O U P I P E T T E G W H R
I Q D B T C H C Y S N O M I Q
```

Complete this classic sudoku grid by filling in the numbers 1–9 so that each row, each column, and each smaller set of 3 x 3 squares contain each number just once and once only.

5		1	8	6			9	7
	8			4			1	
		6	1			5	4	
4	5							
		7		9	4		3	
9	6			1		7		4
7		5		8	2		6	
6		8	4		1			5
		4						

It's Careers Day, and eight pupils—Paula, Quentin, Roberta, Simon, Tim, Uriah, Veronica, and William—have brought one of their parents to school with them to talk about their occupation: one is a veterinarian; one is an accountant; another is a lawyer; another is a piano teacher; one is a librarian; another works in a supermarket; one is a taxicab driver; and another is a personal trainer.

Based on the clues below, can you work out what each pupil's parent does for a living?

1. The librarian and the PT both have daughters.

2. The parent who works in a supermarket has a name four letters longer than the boy whose parent is the piano teacher.

3. The veterinarian's child has a 7-letter name, and the taxicab driver's child has a 5-letter name.

4. Paula's parent is an accountant...

5. ...but Roberta's isn't a librarian, and Uriah's doesn't drive a taxi!

PUPIL	PARENT'S JOB
Paula	
Quentin	
Roberta	
Simon	
Tim	
Uriah	
Veronica	
William	

"I'm sorry I haven't got my homework with me," said the student, "but I did it so well, my mom wanted to..."—what?

In this mega acrostic puzzle, you now have 18 trivia questions to solve. As before, place their answers into the corresponding rows in the grid on the opposite page, and the rest of the student's excuse will be spelled out down the shaded column!

1. In psychology, what is an uncontrollable desire to set fire to things called?

2. What two-word nickname is given to the flag of the United Kingdom? (5,4)

3. Gatlinburg is a city in what landlocked US state?

4. The Komodo dragon and the Sumatran tiger are animals unique to what island nation?

5. What 1937 fantasy novel was subtitled *There and Back Again*? (3,6)

6. By what two-word Latin name is the constellation of the Big Dipper also known? (4,5)

7. Which German composer (surname only) is known for his famous Canon in D written for string quartet?

8. In poetry, what name is given to any stanza or verse form that contains eight lines?

9. The Sandinista National Liberation Front is a politician force in what central American country?

10. What southern arm of the Pacific Ocean—named after a famous Dutch explorer—lies between southeastern Australia and New Zealand? (6,3)

11. What viral inflammatory infection of the liver has varieties designated A, B, and C?

12. In what Scottish city is there a castle built upon the mound of an extinct volcano known as Arthur's Mount?

13. Which Italian mathematician gives his name to a number sequence in which each successive value is the sum of the two previous digits?

14. By what two-word nickname is the planet Mars known, in reference to its rusty appearance?

15. According to an 1890 poem by WB Yeats, the poet will "will arise and go now, and go to"—where?

16. In what athletics discipline is the current word record 9,126 points?

17. What peninsula in northwest Turkey was, in 1915, the site of heavy fighting between Allied and Turkish forces in the First World War?

18. What river, alongside the Tigris, was one of the two great rivers of ancient Mesopotamia?

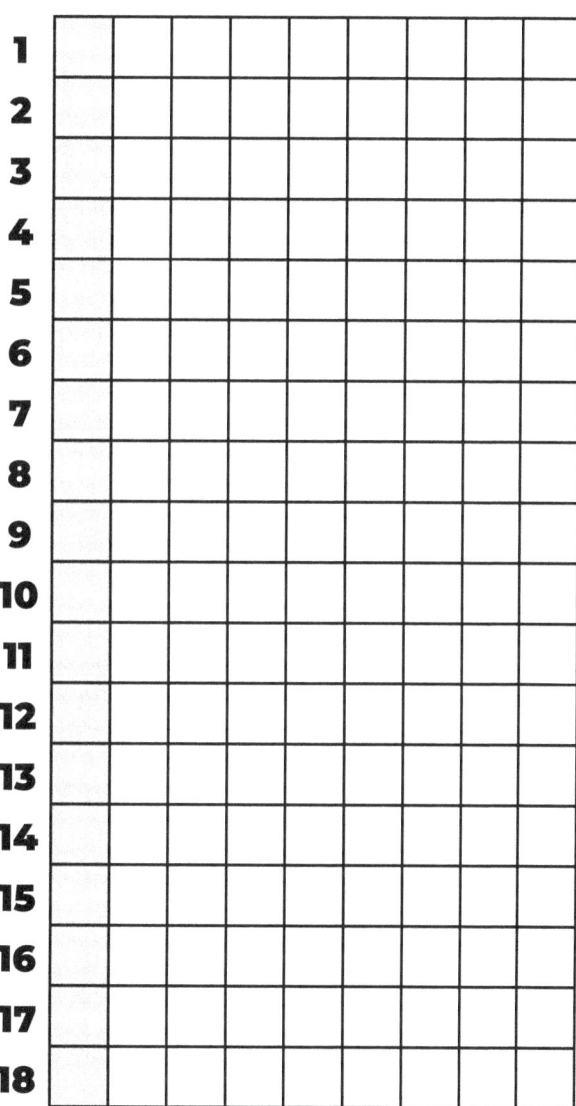

Starting at the 11 in the top left corner here, complete all the squares in the grid below using each of the calculations between them to fill in the gaps.

[11]	×9	[ ]	÷3	[ ]	÷3	[ ]
×8		−9		+12		+9
[ ]	+2	[ ]	÷2	[ ]	−25	[ ]
−68		÷3		+1/3		×4
[ ]	+10	[ ]	×2	[ ]	+1/3	[ ]
×4		×4		−1/3		÷4
[ ]	×1/2	[ ]	/3	[ ]	÷2	[ ]

Here's one final picture puzzle for you.

Are there more correct or incorrect answers in the grid below?

☑ CORRECT   ☒ INCORRECT

CONCLUSION

And with that last test of your mental agility, we've come to an end!

We hope you've enjoyed your Ultimate Teacher's Activity Book—and as well as testing your brainpower, your word power, and your general knowledge along the way, we hope you've learned a thing or too as well!

After all, it's never too late to learn something new—as your students will no doubt be aware!

Time for a well-earned break, now though. So make yourself a drink, put your feet up, and kick back. That marking and lesson planning can wait for another day...

SOLUTIONS

6

```
C H F H V G Y Q E A H R L I T
K G H A C G E C O R E G C F K
A Y Q T O N O O K T J Z O P H
Q M S L A N E S R A B X I L S
R H O Q O M X R C G A J L L I
P I K M O N V C F K R Y E J L
B R I H S I N A P S R A N B G
V C O A M A R D X D M C P U N
S Z N U A O Y V P N G X L H E
H I S T O R Y W C H P D K F Y
O I E F N D I Q K T Y F U D R
C H I S Q M C H E M I S T R Y
P O Q A F U S G P T Q H I A D
C O M P U T E R S C I E N C E
S O C I A L S T U D I E S Z S
```

8

2	3	9	7	1	5	8	6	4
8	6	7	2	4	9	1	3	5
1	5	4	6	3	8	9	7	2
5	7	6	4	9	3	2	1	8
4	8	2	1	7	6	3	5	9
3	9	1	8	5	2	7	4	6
7	2	5	3	8	4	6	9	1
6	4	3	9	2	1	5	8	7
9	1	8	5	6	7	4	2	3

7

S	A	M	U	E	L
P	A	V	L	O	V
E	D	I	S	O	N
L	E	A	G	U	E
L	E	N	N	O	N
I	C	A	R	U	S
N	E	V	A	D	A
G	E	O	R	G	E
T	H	A	M	E	S
E	S	P	A	N	A
S	A	T	U	R	N
T	A	H	I	T	I

Hidden answer: Spelling test

9

STUDENT	EXCUSE
Aaron	Left at grandmother's
Bryan	Dog ate it
Charlie	Thought it was due tomorrow
Darren	Left on school bus
Eddie	Stomachache

10

11

12

There are 16 triangles in total.

13

Elizabeth I = 1603

Marco Polo = 1324

King John = 1216

Charles Dickens = 1870

Queen Victoria = 1901

Joan of Arc = 1431

George Washington = 1799

Christopher Columbus = 1506

14

15

(crossword solution with entries including: MUCHIMPROVED, HOOT, DMINUS, BETTER, MERIT, OUTSTANDING, MUSTTRYHARDER, DISTINCTION, PERCENTILE, HORROR, PASS, PLUS, TOPOFTHECLASS, FAIL, DIPLOMA)

19

C	U	R	A	U	D	I	T	S	S
R	O	T	S	T	A	L	O	E	I
C	I	A	T	C	O	L	R	R	N
H	N	P	I	T	S	S	I	D	G
E	R	A	M	U	N	E	U	M	R
S	T	D	E	O	R	R	W	I	O
A	P	E	T	C	E	S	E	N	O
R	P	M	P	H	O	U	G	G	M
T	R	O	B	A	S	T	A	S	A
M	E	N	T	C	K	N	O	R	P

Answers: Curtain, Auditorium, Dressing room, Stalls, Orchestra pit, Costume department, Prompt corner, Backstage, House, Wings, Apron.

17

The 10 correct states are Delaware, New York, New Hampshire, Rhode Island, South Carolina, Georgia, Pennsylvania, Maryland, Virginia, and North Carolina.

18

There are more drama lessons (20 in total).

20

W	D	F	A	S	O	Y	I	S	C	M	R	X	H	E
R	B	L	L	S	U	U	T	G	A	O	E	Y	A	M
H	E	Y	A	P	I	E	V	N	U	R	L	G	W	Y
U	K	N	D	R	I	M	A	R	O	R	D	Z	T	O
E	N	I	K	N	E	M	O	Y	R	I	N	O	H	F
A	K	Y	B	L	T	G	T	V	E	S	A	B	O	R
E	D	E	O	I	U	L	Z	O	K	O	H	T	R	D
G	C	K	H	P	L	A	K	T	L	N	C	K	N	Q
K	W	W	C	A	Y	Z	F	R	I	W	K	I	E	I
M	E	L	V	I	L	L	E	Y	K	F	N	Q	B	U
H	H	P	X	L	Q	L	H	T	A	L	P	Y	R	Y
D	J	D	B	H	L	B	R	E	G	N	I	L	A	S
S	X	H	R	E	Z	E	C	M	P	K	L	E	Q	H
J	W	X	H	B	E	L	L	O	W	V	Y	Y	W	I
C	D	A	L	J	J	Q	Z	M	U	W	E	L	Z	L

21

STUDENT	SUBJECT
Annie	Geography
Ben	Art
Charles	History
Diedre	Music
Evie	Math

22

4	7	6	9	5	1	2	8	3
3	9	1	8	2	6	4	5	7
2	5	8	4	3	7	9	1	6
5	3	4	1	8	2	7	6	9
1	6	7	3	4	9	8	2	5
8	2	9	6	7	5	1	3	4
9	1	5	2	6	4	3	7	8
7	4	3	5	1	8	6	9	2
6	8	2	7	9	3	5	4	1

23

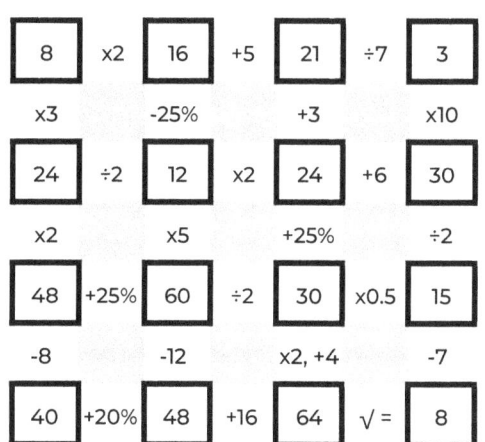

24

25

ATLAS and GLOBE.

26

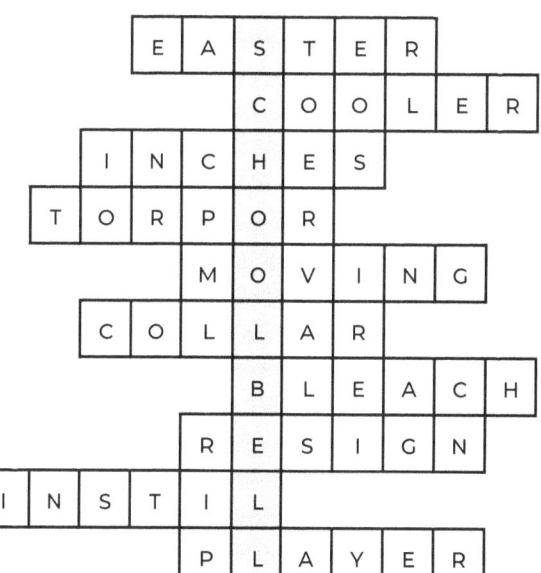

Hidden answer: School bell

27

Shuttlecock = Badminton

Pommel horse = Gymnastics

Mitt = Babeball

Carabiner = Climbing

Racket = Tennis

Shin guard = Soccer

Tee = Golf

Bails = Cricket

30

6	7	2	3	9	1	4	8	5
4	9	1	5	8	6	7	2	3
3	5	8	2	4	7	6	1	9
2	8	9	1	6	4	3	5	7
1	6	3	7	5	8	9	4	2
7	4	5	9	3	2	1	6	8
8	2	7	6	1	3	5	9	4
9	1	4	8	7	5	2	3	6
5	3	6	4	2	9	8	7	1

28

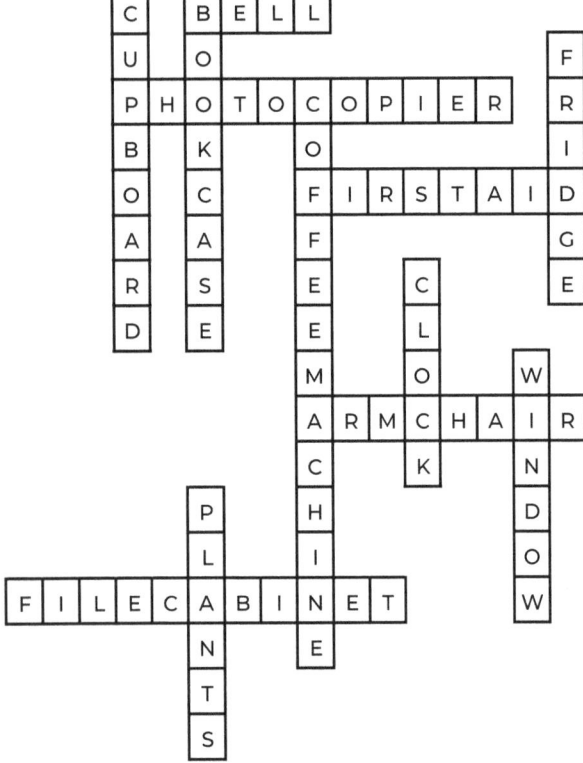

31

C	H	A	P	T	E	R
I	T	A	L	I	A	N
R	U	S	S	I	A	N
C	A	L	G	A	R	Y
U	N	I	C	O	R	N
L	I	B	R	A	R	Y
A	B	R	A	H	A	M
R	I	C	H	A	R	D
S	E	N	E	G	A	L
A	N	T	H	O	N	Y
W	I	N	D	O	W	S

Hidden Answer: Circular saw

32

The playwrights are Eugene O'Neill, Arthur Miller, August Strindberg, GB Shaw, Anton Chekov, Henrik Ibsen, Samuel Beckett, Oscar Wilde, Tennessee Williams, and Berthold Brecht.

33

There are 13 squares in total.

34

CHALKBOARD, BOOKCASE, CHAIRS, TELEVISION, COMPUTER, and CUPBOARD.

35

CLASS	TIME
1A	10am
2B	9am
3C	11am
4D	1pm
5E	2pm

36

```
N X D G H L L J I W D G B E R
Q O N X J P L W S U E E A T B
L B S T A M E I M E L M R N M
J G C V X W R B M G P A S A H
T N Q I H O B B P D M O E O S
R I N G S E J H C P A B R Y P
L T F P L R E W O R E E I K R
L L K L O W R L H C Q B R Q I
E U S Y J M I T N G P J L T N
B A A N T N M A C S S X G U G
R V A E E E L E J X D N G I B
A O M H J A F L L W K W L F O
B F T K B T A Y G U D A P F A
E X E R C I S E B I K E C K R
E M A R F G N I B M I L C K D
```

37

Meringue = Egg whites

Panna cotta = Cream

Gazpacho = Tomato

Hash brown = Potato

Coq au vin = Chicken

Chowder = Seafood

Bibimbap = Rice

Borscht = Beet

38

	S	T	A	T	E		N	U	M	B	S
A		O		O		A		P		U		C
G	E	N	E	R	I	C		S	A	F	E	R
E		I		E		C		T		F		E
N	I	C	E		S	E	P	A	R	A	T	E
T				O		S		R		L		D
	C	O	M	P	O	S	I	T	I	O	N	
T		U		P		O		T				F
O	U	T	D	O	O	R	S		P	U	R	R
T		L		S		I		S		T		E
A	L	I	B	I		E	S	T	A	T	E	S
L		N		T		S		E		E		H
	L	E	V	E	R		S	P	I	R	E	

39

40

"My hand fell asleep and I didn't want to wake it!"

41

42

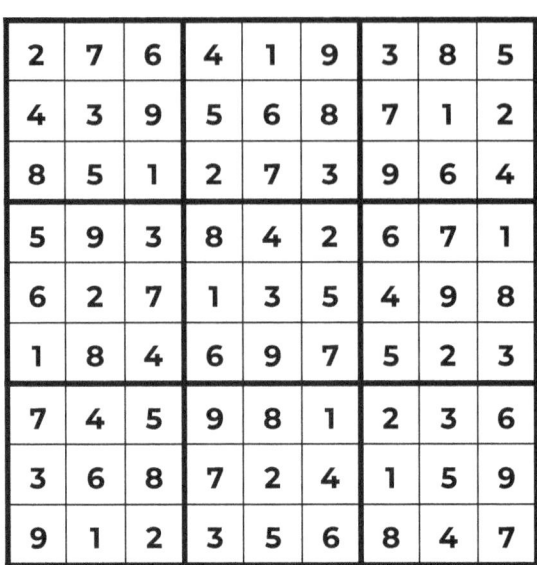

44

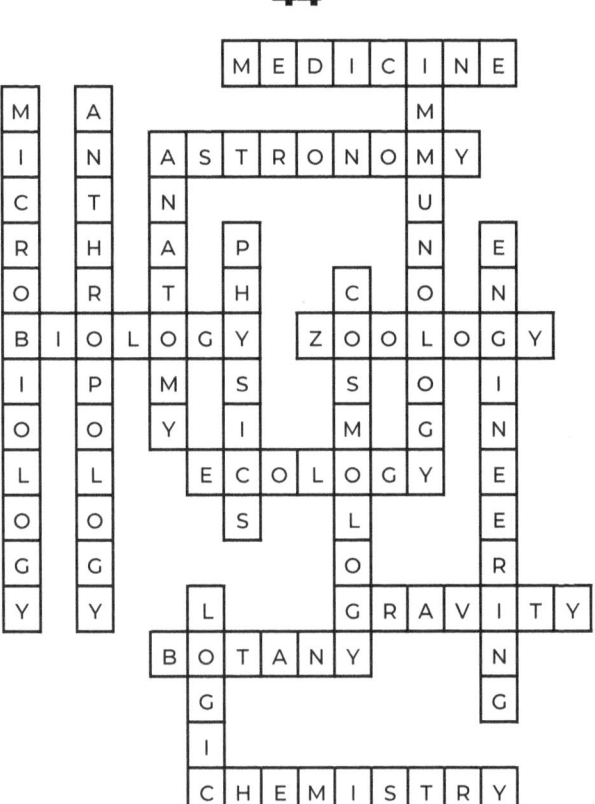

45

D	I	O	D	E
E	G	Y	P	T
T	H	O	T	H
E	A	G	L	E
N	A	N	C	Y
T	E	V	E	T
I	V	O	R	Y
O	M	A	H	A
N	I	X	O	N

Hidden answer: Detention

46

There are more A+ grades (22).

47

48

```
O N O E B C M E N Z D V K A Y
J I Y W A D S A N A V A J O N
I T U U Z E O Q O P I U E A S
B A H R N F W X F O X L I G R
W L Q A R K O K L R F S A Y F
E L P E T P T E L T S B V T T
M A N D A R I N N U L N A B I
J C S A Z I Q L R G F N R R G
H S X H I E J N V U L E D E H
O J C R A G B Z P E C I R U S
H C T U D K E B N S P M S N I
H S I N A P S W P E A X I H K
X M N T B D P H R N Y R V G R
K W O P I R N Q G O L L U B U
E M F M X U D Q E Y N C N T T
```

49

1. KENNEDY and TAFT
2. WASHINGTON and LINCOLN
3. OBAMA and HOOVER
4. ADAMS and HARDING
5. HARRISON and TYLER
6. COOLIDGE and ROOSEVELT
7. VAN BUREN and JACKSON
8. JOHNSON and CLEVELAND

50

The Euro nations are Luxembourg, Cyprus, Estonia, Ireland, Austria, Croatia, Belgium, Slovenia, Finland, and Slovakia. Of the others, Norway, Russia, and Switzerland are not EU members, while both Poland and Bulgaria are EU states that have as yet not adopted the euro.

51

C	L	A	A	T	L	A	E	T	A
E	T	V	P	E	L	M	M	A	T
R	S	I	C	L	E	A	S	R	F
N	S	U	M	U	H	N	U	R	E
U	S	R	E	B	I	D	S	U	M
M	C	E	M	L	T	I	B	I	A
P	A	T	A	E	C	A	L	U	I
U	H	A	C	F	I	A	C	S	D
L	Y	R	P	U	B	N	E	U	A
A	O	I	D	S	U	L	A	S	R

ANSWERS: Clavicle, Patella, Metatarsus, Sternum, Mandible, Femur, Humerus, Scapula, Hyoid, Metacarpus, Fibula, Tibia, Radius, Calcaneus.

52

(crossword with answers: STAPLER, PEN, ERASER, SCISSORS, BOOK, CLIP, SHARPENER, FOLDER, GLUE, PRITT, TAPE, TRACTOR, FASTENER, NOTEBOOK, PENCIL, PENCILCASE, COMPASS, etc.)

54

Gym	Music	Drama	History	Math	Art
History	Art	Math	Gym	Music	Drama
Drama	Math	Art	Music	Gym	History
Music	History	Gym	Drama	Art	Math
Math	Gym	History	Art	Drama	Music
Art	Drama	Music	Math	History	Gym

55

"I didn't do it because I didn't want to add to your workload!"

56

57

1	5	2	9	7	6	8	3	4
8	6	4	2	3	5	9	1	7
7	3	9	4	8	1	6	5	2
5	4	3	6	1	2	7	8	9
2	9	1	7	4	8	3	6	5
6	8	7	3	5	9	4	2	1
3	1	5	8	9	4	2	7	6
9	7	6	5	2	3	1	4	8
4	2	8	1	6	7	5	9	3

58

P	R	O	F	I	T
S	A	H	A	R	A
Y	A	M	A	H	A
C	H	I	R	O	N
H	A	R	R	I	S
O	S	I	R	I	S
L	O	N	D	O	N
O	X	F	O	R	D
G	R	E	E	C	E
Y	E	L	L	O	W

Hidden answer: Psychology

60

TEACHER	LUNCH
Mr. Phips	Chicken soup
Miss Quigley	Lasagna
Mrs. Robinson	Ham quiche
Ms. Simmonds	Mac and cheese
Mr. Thomson	Chicken salad
Mr. Underwood	Cheese sandwich

61

L	L	A	H	G	N	I	N	I	D	M	N	L	K	S
S	L	A	P	I	C	N	I	R	P	O	M	K	R	M
D	C	V	C	N	G	K	J	V	P	O	P	E	D	O
N	O	I	T	P	E	C	E	R	P	R	K	L	E	O
R	M	F	E	O	M	Y	K	S	M	C	G	I	T	R
E	N	H	D	N	N	U	T	M	O	I	D	B	E	S
T	L	G	R	P	C	A	I	L	F	S	A	R	N	S
A	N	M	U	R	F	E	I	S	E	U	H	A	T	A
E	B	E	A	F	N	H	L	I	A	M	H	R	I	L
H	A	H	R	U	C	W	W	A	Y	N	E	Y	O	C
T	X	O	E	H	C	D	L	F	B	O	M	F	N	P
M	O	O	R	Y	D	U	T	S	N	B	F	Y	A	F
M	G	I	L	Q	A	R	T	R	O	O	M	J	G	S
C	H	A	N	G	I	N	G	R	O	O	M	S	E	V
K	Q	T	X	D	N	F	E	C	I	F	F	O	X	L

62

Banquo = Macbeth

Oberon = A Midsummer Night's Dream

Viola = Twelfth Night

Brutus = Julius Caesar

Cordelia = King Lear

Prospero = The Tempest

Katherine = The Taming of the Shrew

Ophelia = Hamlet

63

64

The correct elements are carbon, astatine, boron, manganese, arsenic, zinc, iodine, tungsten, tin, and iron.

65

There are 12 squares in total.

66

The dishes on the menu are HAMBURGER, MAC AND CHEESE, SPAGHETTI, CHICKEN SOUP, and CHEESE SALAD.

67

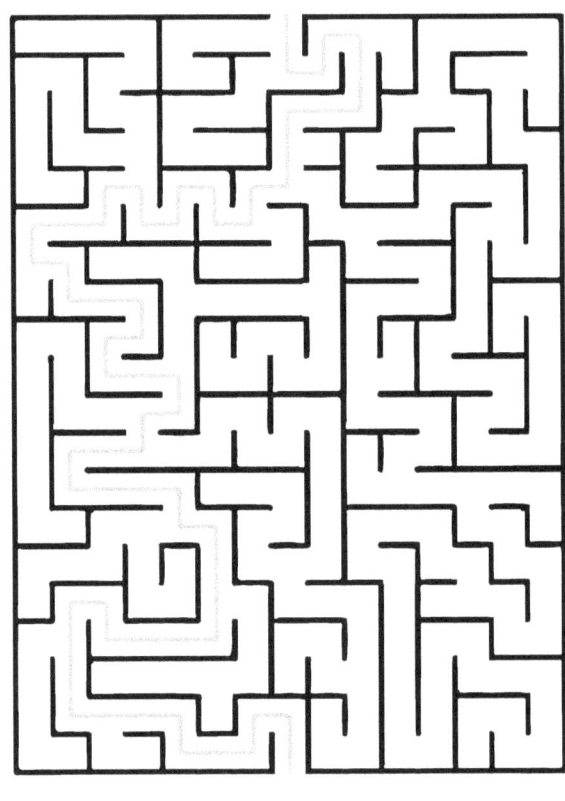

68

"My cat ate it, knowing that I'd blame the dog instead."

69

The books are GREAT EXPECTATIONS, TO KILL A MOCKINGBIRD, THE BELL JAR, and WUTHERING HEIGHTS.

70

6	×4	24	÷3	8	+7	10
-4		-4		×5		×0.5
2	×10	20	×2	40	÷8	5
×11		+24		×2.2		×20
22	×2	44	×2	88	+12	100
-17		-14		-28		√=
5	×6	30	×2	60	÷6	10

72

6	7	2	8	4	9	1	5	3
3	1	5	2	6	7	4	8	9
4	9	8	5	3	1	6	2	7
8	2	7	1	9	6	5	3	4
1	4	3	7	2	5	8	9	6
5	6	9	3	8	4	2	7	1
2	8	4	9	1	3	7	6	5
9	5	1	6	7	2	3	4	8
7	3	6	4	5	8	9	1	2

73

STUDENT	ROLE
Jamie	Fagin
Kenny	Artful Dodger
Linda	Oliver
Marina	Nancy
Owen	Chorus
Philip	Bill Sykes

74

C	A	N	A	D	I	A	N
L	I	N	G	E	R	I	E
E	N	O	L	A	G	A	Y
V	I	R	G	I	N	I	A
E	T	H	I	O	P	I	A
R	U	T	A	B	A	G	A
E	U	R	Y	D	I	C	E
R	A	S	P	U	T	I	N
T	E	N	N	Y	S	O	N
H	A	R	R	I	S	O	N
E	M	M	A	N	U	E	L
N	I	T	R	O	G	E	N

Hidden answer: Cleverer then!

75

Botany = Plants

Mycology = Fungi

Optics = Light

Astronomy = Space

Seismology = Earthquakes

Glaciology = Ice

Paleontology = Fossils

Acoustics = Sound

Hydrology = Water

76

The square numbers are 225 (15), 289 (17), 169 (13), 196 (14), 961 (31), 256 (16), 900 (30), 100 (10), 676 (26), and 441 (21).

78

```
L L A B T O O F R L P I T B L
T E R R A S T G L E S Z B Z L
D V A G R K Q A H O C K E Y A
L C O M C R B X N O Y C J O B
K U C K H Y W T B Q O B O D T
X E X R E M D R T W M R G S E
C S P L R T U S E C X A C U N
Z S L U Y C E X R S D I P A R
L O J S C I T E L H T A G T E
V R T L U I D K U S H L U J F
D C U E J N R K A Y M D I B G
E A K G N X U N S L S Y G N A
F L F W G N M S W I M M I N G
D Y T K B Y I L L A B T F O S
P D X A G Y S S R Q H R E Q H
```

79

There are more brushes—20 in total.

80

81

SMALL and LARGE.

82

83

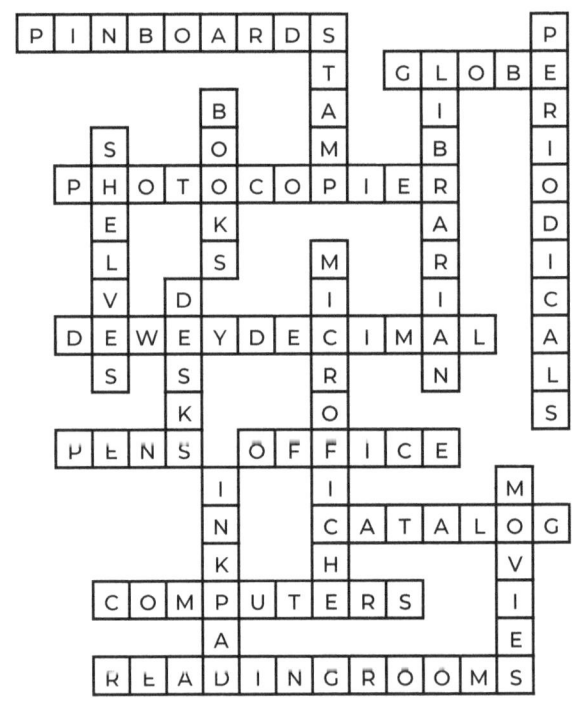

84

S	I	S	T	E	R		F		S		M
T		H		X		L	O	C	A	T	E	D
A	D	U	L	T	S		R		F		S
M		F		I		B	E	C	A	U	S	E
I	N	F	A	N	T		V		R		A
N		L		C			E		I		G
A	C	E		T	H	E	R	E		B	E	G
		H		S		O		X		R		A
		R		O		R		S	T	E	A	M	S
C	O	N	C	E	R	T		R		V		P
		N		I			S	A	L	A	M	I
G	I	R	A	F	F	E		C		D		N
		C		L		Y		S	T	R	O	N	G

85

1	6	3	4	5	9	7	8	2
7	2	4	1	8	3	6	5	9
5	8	9	2	7	6	3	4	1
9	3	7	6	4	8	2	1	5
8	1	2	5	9	7	4	3	6
6	4	5	3	2	1	9	7	8
4	5	6	8	3	2	1	9	7
3	7	1	9	6	5	8	2	4
2	9	8	7	1	4	5	6	3

86

PUPIL	TOPIC
David	Reading
Erica	Fishing
Fabien	Ballet
Georgia	Bird watching
Harrison	Baseball
India	Science fiction

87

P	A	N	D	A
E	I	G	H	T
N	E	P	A	L
C	A	N	I	S
I	T	A	L	Y
L	U	Z	O	N
C	H	E	S	S
A	T	L	A	S
S	E	V	E	N
E	B	O	N	Y

Hidden answer: Pencil case

88

1. ALGEBRA and EQUATION
2. REHEARSAL and SCRIPT
3. ATOM and ELECTRON
4. ATLAS and CLIMATE
5. GRAMMAR and PROSE
6. CELL and MEMBRANE
7. PORTRAIT and SCULPTURE
8. ALKALI and ELEMENT

89

The correct 20th century figures are Edward VIII (d.1972), Mother Theresa (d. 1997), Albert Einstein (d. 1955), Mahatma Gandhi (d. 1948), Robert Falcon Scott (d. 1912), Winston Churchill (d. 1965), Lizzie Borden (d. 1927), Pablo Picasso (d. 1973), Emmeline Pankhurst (d. 1928), and John Dillinger (d. 1934).

90

W	H	I	Y	E	A	T	N	O	T
I	D	T	O	R	F	S	L	P	L
C	A	M	S	T	G	N	I	I	I
K	N	O	N	E	M	E	R	K	M
I	Y	R	S	Y	N	O	S	E	G
N	B	H	O	N	D	O	N	N	N
S	O	T	N	N	Y	B	R	N	I
H	N	A	L	E	E	W	O	W	H
U	E	S	P	T	L	O	S	W	T
G	H	S	H	E	L	R	D	O	R

The answers are Whitman, Yeats, Milton, Frost, Dickinson, Byron, Kipling, Emerson, Hughes, Plath, Shelly, Donne, Browning, and Wordsworth.

91

X	Q	J	Y	I	S	H	G	R	I	S	N	B	H	S
S	J	Y	T	M	P	L	O	A	P	E	K	N	C	E
M	Z	D	F	P	R	B	A	O	W	A	X	P	P	M
X	W	U	O	R	E	H	R	S	K	M	H	L	L	U
H	C	T	T	O	M	P	F	I	R	C	O	E	E	T
C	C	S	Z	V	I	B	P	A	U	A	A	H	B	S
P	A	R	T	S	E	H	C	R	O	D	E	Z	O	O
R	S	E	Z	L	R	M	T	N	R	H	I	H	S	C
O	M	D	X	U	E	A	X	O	A	W	D	M	E	Y
G	H	N	F	D	I	P	L	A	C	I	S	U	M	R
R	L	U	P	N	C	E	R	E	Y	S	N	P	H	V
A	L	P	C	P	E	R	F	O	R	M	A	N	C	E
M	U	A	L	I	N	E	S	C	M	F	K	H	A	Q
A	L	G	N	I	T	S	A	C	X	P	B	K	D	P
L	U	R	N	O	P	Q	V	N	M	B	T	R	L	X

92

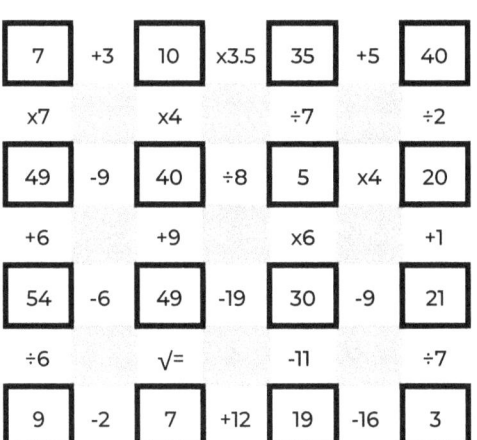

93

97

EROSION
RIVER
PERCOLATION
GROUNDWATER
LAKE
WATERTABLE
PRECIPITATION
AQUIFER
CONDENSATION
SNOW
SEA
EVAPORATION
SNOWMELT
TRANSPIRATION
RAIN
INFILTRATION
RUNOFF
FOG

95

There are more left-handed students (30).

96

Mercury = 1st

Venus = 2nd

Earth = 3rd

Mars = 4th

Jupiter = 5th

Saturn = 6th

Uranus = 7th

Neptune = 8th

98

2	5	8	6	4	1	7	9	3
6	7	9	3	2	8	1	4	5
4	3	1	7	9	5	6	8	2
3	2	7	1	8	9	5	6	4
5	1	6	2	3	4	8	7	9
9	8	4	5	6	7	3	2	1
1	9	2	8	7	3	4	5	6
8	4	5	9	1	6	2	3	7
7	6	3	4	5	2	9	1	8

99

PUPIL	ADDRESS
Alice	South Avenue
Beatrice	West Road
Christopher	High Street
Daniel	Main Street
Edgar	North Road
Fred	Front Street
Greta	East Avenue

100

W	A	L	T	E	R	R	A	L	E	I	G	H
O	T	T	O	M	A	N	E	M	P	I	R	E
R	E	N	E	D	E	S	C	A	R	T	E	S
L	I	E	C	H	T	E	N	S	T	E	I	N
D	E	C	O	R	A	T	I	O	N	D	A	Y
A	L	P	H	A	C	E	N	T	A	U	R	I
T	R	I	N	I	T	Y	S	U	N	D	A	Y
L	E	S	M	I	S	E	R	A	B	L	E	S
A	T	L	A	N	T	I	C	O	C	E	A	N
S	A	M	U	E	L	B	E	C	K	E	T	T

Hidden answer: World atlas

102

L	O	W		F		A	I	R
O		H	A	L	L	S		A
S	H	E		O		H	I	C
E		N	E	W	L	Y		E
			R		A			
S		M	A	Y	B	E		S
P	O	E		A		N	E	T
O		A	I	R	E	D		U
T	A	N		D		S	A	D

103

"I did it, but I didn't write it down. It's all in my head!"

104

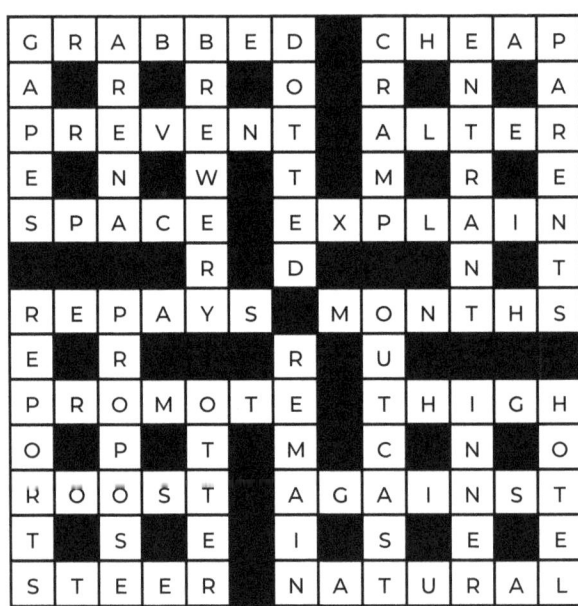

105

Birmingham = Montgomery (Alabama)
Jacksonville = Tallahassee (Florida)
Wilmington = Dover (Delaware)
Anchorage = Juneau (Alaska)
Omaha = Lincoln (Nebraska)
Milwaukee = Madison (Wisconsin)
Portland = Salem (Oregon)
Fargo = Bismarck (North Dakota)

106

107

The correct units of length and distance are league, mile, light year, furlong, chain, cable, yard, parsec, angstrom, and decameter.

109

M	A	C	C	O	R	I	O	L	A
C	Y	D	U	F	I	L	O	U	N
B	M	M	A	F	V	I	S	S	T
E	O	V	L	L	A	A	U	T	I
L	L	I	O	Y	D	C	A	L	I
I	N	E	T	M	M	E	R	C	B
K	H	A	Y	A	C	I	A	U	A
C	E	I	B	T	B	A	G	T	N
O	R	M	A	L	E	I	O	I	O
L	Y	H	S	H	T	T	R	O	P

ANSWERS: Macduff, Coriolanus, Cymbeline, Olivia, Caliban, Malvolio, Tybalt, Hermia, Shylock, Lady Macbeth, Iago, Portia, and Mercutio.

110

Y	Z	R	C	S	Z	T	B	G	N	X	W	K	C	R
I	L	L	F	O	O	B	A	E	S	E	E	U	E	L
U	I	O	N	N	S	S	C	A	V	S	T	U	R	
P	G	Y	G	Q	T	I	H	L	L	K	E	N	E	P
E	H	S	G	A	R	H	C	Y	A	M	E	P	U	U
T	T	G	P	O	V	R	P	A	O	I	A	R	G	B
T	E	S	T	T	U	B	E	M	L	P	V	L	X	K
E	R	F	Q	J	N	G	R	T	S	F	K	J	P	A
R	D	U	J	K	J	E	N	U	G	O	L	Y	W	I
U	L	M	R	O	H	O	M	U	U	Z	E	A	V	F
B	A	E	E	T	N	T	O	O	P	B	E	V	S	B
B	H	H	N	F	I	R	E	P	P	O	R	D	Y	K
E	Y	O	R	L	E	P	O	C	S	O	R	C	I	M
X	T	O	U	P	I	P	E	T	T	E	G	W	H	R
I	Q	D	B	T	C	H	C	Y	S	N	O	M	I	Q

111

5	4	1	8	6	3	2	9	7
2	8	9	7	4	5	3	1	6
3	7	6	1	2	9	5	4	8
4	5	3	2	7	6	1	8	9
8	1	7	5	9	4	6	3	2
9	6	2	3	1	8	7	5	4
7	3	5	9	8	2	4	6	1
6	2	8	4	3	1	9	7	5
1	9	4	6	5	7	8	2	3

113

PUPIL	PARENT'S JOB
Paula	Accountant
Quentin	Veterinarian
Roberta	Personal trainer
Simon	Taxicab driver
Tim	Piano teacher
Uriah	Lawyer
Veronica	Librarian
William	Supermarket

115

P	Y	R	O	M	A	N	I	A
U	N	I	O	N	J	A	C	K
T	E	N	N	E	S	S	E	E
I	N	D	O	N	E	S	I	a
T	H	E	H	O	B	B	I	T
U	R	S	A	M	A	J	O	R
P	A	C	H	E	L	B	E	L
O	C	T	A	S	T	I	C	H
N	I	C	A	R	A	G	U	A
T	A	S	M	A	N	S	E	A
H	E	P	A	T	I	T	I	S
E	D	I	N	B	U	R	G	H
F	I	B	O	N	A	C	C	I
R	E	D	P	L	A	N	E	T
I	N	N	I	S	F	R	E	E
D	E	C	A	T	H	L	O	N
G	A	L	L	I	P	O	L	I
E	U	P	H	R	A	T	E	S

Hidden answer: Put it up on the fridge!

116

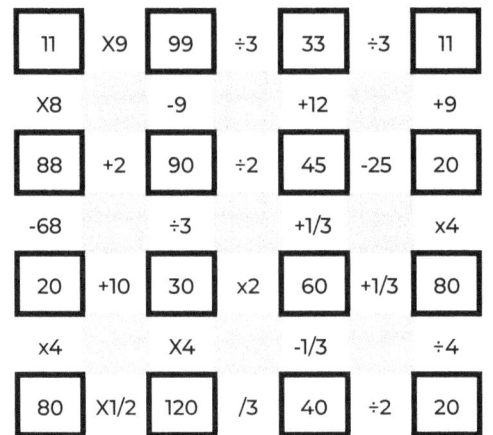

117

There are more correct answers (29).

www.ingramcontent.com/pod-product-compliance
Lightning Source LLC
Chambersburg PA
CBHW081159020426
42333CB00020B/2557